For
Big Bucks
Only

For Big Bucks Only

Hunter's Information Series™
North American Hunting Club
Minneapolis, Minnesota

For Big Bucks Only

Library of Congress Catalog Card Number 87-63364
ISBN 0-914697-17-X

Printed in U.S.A.
    3 4 5 6 7 8 9

Contents

Acknowledgments

The author would like to extend a special thank you to his wife, Corie, for her patience and honest criticism, and to Arvo Hoppala, the successful big buck hunter who shared his secrets with the author.

Thanks also to the NAHC staff for their behind-the-scene work: Publisher Mark LaBarbera, Editor Bill Miller, Associate Editor Dan Dietrich, Editorial Assistants Karyl Dodge and Debra Morem, Member Products Manager Mike Vail and Special Projects Coordinator Linda Kalinowski.

Steven F. Burke, President
North American Hunting Club

Photo Credits

All of the photos in this book were provided by the author. In addition to examples of his own talent, he has included photos from Mike Biggs, Judd Cooney, Craig Cousins, Mark LaBarbera, Leonard Lee Rue Enterprises, Mark Pittman, Dean Reidt, Kumler's Taxidermy, William Vaznis, C.E. Peel, Irene Vandermolen and Westervelt Lodge.

About The Author

To know Jeff Murray is to read his writings. His very heart and soul bleed through the words because he never holds anything back. Murray isn't much of a man-pleaser. Early on he learned that he's not very good at being someone he's not. But he's very good at being himself.

Jeff Murray is not a whitetail pro. He doesn't sell scents or promote hunting gadgets. What he does promote, however, are the golden nuggets of truth he's discovered about his favorite pastime—deer hunting.

Whether it's traipsing the countryside for shed antlers, or researching the latest professional journal, Murray is constantly curious. Perhaps his greatest asset is his ability to integrate wildlife research with personal outdoor observations and experiences. As a former environmental planner, Murray is adept at translating complex biological concepts into practical, in-the-field strategies.

This is no flippant statement. It takes a rare individual to pull this off. Why? Hard-core science often conflicts with cherished whitetail dogma. And while many whitetail authorities are interested mainly in the whens, wheres and hows, finding out the *whys* is the real key to understanding trophy white-tailed deer.

Unfortunately, trailing whys can be frustrating. Dead ends and circular routes that lead back to Square One abound. It takes a certain diligence and commitment—make that passion—to tread

forward in the whitetail game. Especially when tradition says, "Stop here." If you're Jeff Murray, you can't stop. You must go on.

Incentives help. Bagging a mature buck is rewarding, and Murray has done it. He has successfully hunted big bucks throughout Canada and the U.S., with exceptional success in the Midwest.

Few people earn their entire living by pursuing their heart's desire. When they do, the results are often extraordinary. Welcome to the world of an unassuming full-time whitetail nut.

Dedication

To my heavenly Father, who has given me an insatiable thirst for truth.

To Len, my brother-in-law—may he profit from the contents of this book. And to Myles Keller and Noble Carlson, two authentic trophy hunters who really know what big bucks are all about.

Foreword

When Jeff Murray agreed to write this book for North American Hunting Club members, we were delighted. As a fellow hunter and a professional outdoor communicator, he knows how to identify the most important information hidden in the success stories told by expert whitetail hunters. And he knows how to share these valuable hints and tips in the most enlightening way.

Some of the most successful experts in any field have what they call an indescribable knack for doing the right thing at the right time; they can't explain how they consistently outperform the rest of us, but they continue to capture the spotlight. And sometimes the most successful guys prefer to stay hidden from the spotlight, finding solitude and satisfaction in their silent success.

Well, Jeff Murray digs deep to discover the real secrets behind the success of hunting's greatest whitetail men. One of them is in the spotlight. The other is one of the silent success stories.

Jeff learns from listening to these two experts and many other whitetail authorities, and then he describes for all NAHC members how you can be as successful as Myles Keller and Noble Carlson.

By paying attention to details and putting into practice the secrets Jeff and the NAHC have captured for you in this volume, soon you too will be hunting successfully *"For Big Bucks Only."*

Mark LaBarbera
Publisher

Introduction

Big bucks are different. If they weren't, they'd never make it past year two when their headgear begins to show. By the same token, successful hunters of big bucks are different. And the techniques they use to harvest big bucks are different from those most sportsmen use to hunt big deer.

This book uncovers those techniques and explores the three elements of big buck hunting: scouting, location and tactics.

Take scouting. Most everyone knows what topographical maps look like, as well as how to read the contours. But few realize that there's a much better map available for doing accurate field reconnaissance. It's so effective, that in many cases you can find a deer hotspot without stepping into the woods. It's called a stereoscopic map. Stereoscopy lets you see ground cover *three-dimensionally*. Chapter 1 details what you need to know about these maps to use them effectively, from the basics to quite a few fine points. Your scouting will never be the same.

Chapter 2 describes a scouting method that will allow you to keep tabs on the local deer herd while other hunters seem to lag one step behind. It's the acorn connection, and there are some things you must know to hunt deer in the acorns with consistent results. This chapter answers questions such as: Which species of oak do deer prefer? How do deer respond to acorn crops? How do does differ from bucks in their response to mast crop failure?

In Chapter 3 you'll find that I've uncovered the ultimate secret when it comes to scouting big buck country. No, it's not scrapes, but rubs. I've dug out the very latest research on rubs, and there are some interesting insights to be gleaned here. For instance, did you know that a September rub can tell you much more about a big buck's whereabouts than one made in October or November? And did you know that there's a specific rub one researcher discovered that should definitely be hunted over, because a big buck is likely to return to it several times during the rutting season? Furthermore, rubs apparently determine when does go into estrus, and thus, the exact timing of the rut. This chapter, "Rub Your Buck The Right Way," is sure to be one of the most challenging you've read in a long, long time.

Consider location. Besides scouting, any deer hunter worth his broadheads or bullets needs to accomplish one very simple task. He needs to find deer. However for the vast majority, it's not that simple. What they usually find are more hunters than deer. If this sounds familiar, take a close look at Chapters 4, 5, 6 and 7. I've learned about some nifty places where you can find deer—places that other hunters pass by or don't take the time to uncover. And many of them are little pockets that are close to the home of the average North American Hunting Club member. That's especially good news for the bowhunter who typically enjoys an extended season and would like to pick a pocket or two after work without blowing a lot of precious vacation time.

I'm not going to mention any such places right here. I'd rather you chew on Chapters 4 through 7, and ruminate on them real good. See if they bring to mind something in your own backyard. I'd lay odds they will.

Consider tactics. Once you've done your scouting and located your deer, you've got to match the right tactic to the conditions at hand. This is an important principle, something that seems to escape the average hunter who has yet to shoot a really big buck.

Stand hunting can be almost foolproof for the person who executes all the basics, and doesn't overlook the fine points. Chapter 8 covers both in detail.

Chapter 9 takes stand hunting in cold weather a step further. Again, there's some solid—and very interesting—research that lays a good foundation as to how to beat the cold. I was very fortunate to be able to interview nationally acclaimed hypothermia expert, Dr. Robert Pozos. His insights have saved many a chilling outing for me. I can think of more than one heavy-beamed buck that would have never ended up on the meat pole, had I gotten off my stand to warm up.

Perhaps the ultimate stand hunter is Myles Keller. All he's done is arrowed close to two dozen Pope & Young whitetails. You know luck has nothing to do with it. There's a reason for this man's amazing track record, and in Chapter 10 we get a chance to pick apart his overall hunting strategy. See if your standards stand up to his.

There's a lot more to stand hunting than climbing a tree and hoping a buck saunters by. Chapter 11 is the culmination of over 10 years of my messing around with a unique strategy that works in homogeneous, dense cover in big woods. You probably know what I'm talking about: The deer bed, feed and breed in basically the same area, and there's no discernible travel patterns worth intercepting. My solution? Hunt with a couple of other guys, and exchange stands at prescribed times. You will be able to reap the benefits of silent stand hunting, sneaking stillhunting (between stand locations) and productive driving (deer will be routinely pushed to one another). Read this chapter carefully, because there are more things that can go wrong than a house full of kids left to their own devices. My process of elimination, however, has already worked out the bugs, and it should save you a lot of time and frustration.

But stand hunting isn't the only way to take a trophy buck. Sneaking, stalking and tracking can be just as effective. If you've been reluctant to leave your stand, try easing into one of these methods when the weather is foul. Deer won't be moving, anyway, and you'll only end up wasting time back on that stand. It isn't quite that simple, of course. Deer react in varying ways to weather changes, and the astute hunter knows this. Chapters 12 and 13 delve into the subject of wind, rain, fog and snow in detail. Don't ever let changing weather ruin your game plan again.

Then there's Noble Carlson. What Myles Keller is to bowhunting, Carlson is to hunting whitetails with a gun. He does it all the same way: by tracking. If you think tracking is reserved for a few gifted old-timers you're wrong. You, too, can track bucks, and Chapters 14 and 15 tell you exactly how to do it. In fact, after you read this material, you should be able to distinguish a buck's print from a doe's 100 percent of the time, given adequate snow conditions. If that sounds outlandish, it's only because there's been too much misleading literature printed on the subject by naive outdoor writers. I know, because I was one of them.

Sometimes you try everything in your bag of tricks to get a handle on a big buck's core area, and you end up with deer track soup. There's a little-known tactic that works when all else fails: backtracking. If you can't tell where a buck is, try finding out where he used to be. Then you'll at least have a few clues as to where to concentrate. There are a few tricks to this method, though. Read about them in Chapter 16. Then give the method a shot.

With all this information on big buck hunting, you're going to be tagging lots of big deer. So the final chapter is intended to answer the age-old question of how big that buck you've just downed really is. Because few hunters have the luxury of carting their quarry off to a butcher's scale, Chapter 17 includes several formulas for determining a buck's dressed weight, live weight and expected "freezer weight." Now there are a number of commercially-available "deer tapes" on the market all purporting to estimate these weights. Some are fairly accurate in certain instances. Others are a shot in the dark. The problem is a simple one. Deer body-weights vary considerably from subspecies to subspecies (there are over 30 in the United States) and in various geographic regions. I've done the research and you benefit.

Good hunting.

Jeff Murray

1

A New Dimension
In Deer Scouting

The area looked ideal, just as I had expected. Deer sign abounded along the edge of the swamp and on the hardwood ridge overlooking the beaver pond. At the trickling outlet, where the dam stretched for nearly 100 yards, there were five trails fresh with tracks.

I had seen enough. The adrenaline was already beginning to flow. My hands were all thumbs, but I somehow managed to set up my portable tree stand, without too much noise, in the most obvious spot—below the dam and between the trails.

It was a good choice. In less than 15 minutes, two does came sloshing down the trail immediately below my stand. I raised my Oneida Eagle compound to practice picking a spot, and neither deer flinched.

It's hard to believe that my newfound gold mine was discovered without my setting foot in the woods. It was the easiest find I'd ever made. Unfortunately, a busy fall schedule prevented me from returning with my bow, but that perfect bottleneck produced a nice eight-pointer later on in the firearms season.

How did I find it? A hot tip?

Sort of. As a former environmental planner, I had used a tool of the trade for identifying environmentally sensitive areas. It works just as well for finding legitimate big buck hotspots. So, when I was told that a certain area held big bucks, it was simply a matter of first doing the paperwork.

The "tool" is a stereoscope, which applies the principles of binocular vision so that objects from maps can be viewed three-dimensionally. The stereoscope has two lenses, one for each eye, that are placed directly over a pair of maps. One of your eyes focuses through one lens at one of the maps, while the other eye simultaneously does the same with the second map. It's a nifty system that's irreplaceable to planners, foresters, engineers, mining companies, soil scientists and even the United States military. But it remains relatively unknown to many hunters.

The discipline of remote sensing—examining photographic images for the purpose of identifying objects—can be a real boon for hunters everywhere.

Most of us already have a background in remote sensing. Many hunters use topographic maps that show elevation with contour lines. Indeed, they are helpful, to a point. But topo maps have "a lot of slop and are often misleading," said Dr. Gordon Levine, a former university level geography professor. Topo maps are also limited in the amount of information they can provide. For instance, they cannot tell you whether a certain patch of high ground is a stand of oak (possibly loaded with acorns) or birch; or if a swamp is cedar (deer wintering grounds) or tag alder. And the scale used in most topo maps is very small, which limits the amount of landform detail.

Obviously, the more accurate the information you take into the woods with you—terrain, forest cover, vegetation types, water courses—the less time your field reconnaissance will take. But even more important, an inadequate map could cause you to pass up the hotspot that holds the area's biggest bucks.

Aerial photos are another tool used by professionals and hunters alike. They can give additional clues to ground cover when used in conjunction with contour maps. One trick is to obtain an aerial shot at the same scale as a topo map (the photos are relatively easy and cheap to enlarge or reduce to the proper scale if the same scale is not available). Then, simply overlay the two on a light table or against a living room window. Together, they can tell you things that either map alone would miss.

But this process is far from perfect. Aerial photos can be difficult to interpret, especially if you aren't familiar with the area in question. The chief problem associated with most aerial photographs—as well as topo maps—is how they're taken: from 90

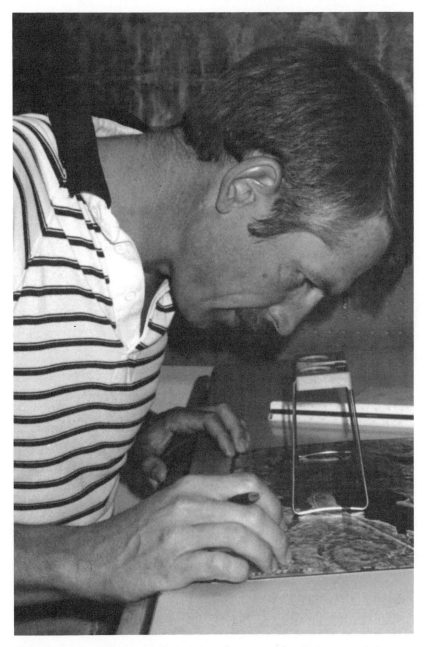

Using stereoscopic maps, a technique usually reserved for engineers and planners, many hunters locate areas that funnel deer through a concentrated lane.

degree projections by aircraft. This only gives you flat, one-dimensional information about the ground surface.

Wouldn't it be nice to know what's under the canopy of the tree growth? An area may appear to be good deer habitat, but the forest floor could be too sparse. The deer may avoid this particular cover during daylight hours. And if there is no food available, that's strike two. Strike three is the distortion involved with standard aerial photographs. Vertical shots taken from the air are accurate and sharp only in the center; the edges of the photograph are often out of focus and not to scale.

There is a better way. When two images of the same area are photographed from different points in the air, they can provide a three-dimensional picture when viewed through a stereoscope. Now, features that lie under the tree cover can be readily identified, plus the types of trees are more easily identified in three-dimensional stereoscopy.

There are three basic types of stereoscopes: pocket, mirror and prism. I use the pocket type because it only costs around $10 and works well enough for my purposes. For years, I used the pair that belonged to the map provider, whether it was a federal or local unit of government or a private institution.

How can you take advantage of stereoscopy locally? Surprisingly, there are more outlets than you would think. Many federal agencies have complete sets of overlapping stereo maps for their particular jurisdiction. For example, if an area you are interested in is within a national forest, look to the U.S. Forest Service. I used the Superior National Forest's map system to locate the beaver pond area mentioned earlier. Planning a trophy mule deer or elk hunt? Consider the Bureau of Land Management for Western lands.

Farm-country whitetails can be mapped out in stereo, too. Many areas of the country, through the Department of Agriculture, are mapped for soil identification. The Agricultural Stabilization and Conservation Service has reactivated an extensive air photo program in farming states. Also, your regional Environmental Protection Agency office, which is interested in protecting valuable wetlands, may be a good source.

State sources are plentiful, too. The state geological survey is a sure bet, but the first place to check would be the wildlife or forestry division of your state's department of natural resources. In fact, many field offices near huntable areas use this mapping tool. And don't forget the transportation department. It relies on remote

You can locate swamp islands and little-known hiding spots for big bucks like this using stereoscopic maps, but you have to be careful not to spook your trophy. Fortunately, the deer observed in these remote hideouts are less jittery than in areas with more hunting pressure.

sensing for routing new right-of-ways through forested areas. State planning agencies may have the most useful maps of all because they need to identify dwellings as well as landforms; the scale of their map systems could be the most useful of all—ranging from 1:1 to 1:12,000.

A good local source is your county's government center or courthouse. The agency to call on would be the planning department or the land commissioner's office. Smaller counties typically contract for services with private companies. The Yellow Pages should list private companies under ''Aerial Aviation'' or ''Planning Consultants.'' Local educational sources include universities, libraries and vocational-technical institutes. Utility companies, to comply with federal mandates, usually keep an aerial-photo mapping system, too. Most public agencies employ a number of qualified individuals trained in aerial-photo interpretation. And they are usually quite agreeable to helping the general public, which is a good thing because using a pocket stereoscope for the first time isn't as easy as it may sound.

However, there may be situations in which you're on your own. A private corporation may not be in a position to provide assistance without a fee. Or a public official may be too busy. Then, you need to know the basic principles of aerial-photo interpretation and how to use a stereoscope. Although I benefited from college coursework that was a requirement for my degree, I still keep a handbook of notes in my "deer file." Included are interpretation pointers that have helped out on several occasions for identifying troublesome landmarks.

I recall one situation in which my neighbor, Tom Long, and I had studied a topographic quadrangle map in search of a swamp island—a patch of high ground surrounded by wetlands. It's one of our surefire hotspots when hunter pressure pushes deer into areas where redcoats won't or can't go.

"I don't know," Tom said. "The island looks too small to hold many bucks."

"But look at the scale—1:24,000," I said. "That means that an inch equals .38 of a mile. I'd say that knoll is at least two acres."

Then, we looked at plain aerial photos. Sure enough, the island was big enough and appeared to have some cover. We were sure that the stereo maps would tell us just how thick it was, and what type of cover it provided. In the past, I've even identified deer trails leading out of bogs with the stereoscope, so I thought that it would be duck soup.

But it wasn't. We didn't get very far because the photos were taken on a cloudy day, and there were no shadows providing the kind of detail we needed. But we didn't give up. I looked in my handbook for shades, textures and tones similar to the ones at which we were looking. In the stereoscope, they looked like aspen saplings and dogwoods, with a few mature oaks. Any big buck on that little knoll would have a perfect sanctuary that provided both security and food.

The final step was to actually scout the area. If it didn't look inviting, we would have simply continued our search for a better

One of the author's favorite hotspots to find big bucks, like this one that Myles Keller arrowed, is on a patch of high ground surrounded by swamps. Stereoscopic maps are ideal for finding these swamp islands.

one. But when Tom checked it out, he found so many deer trails that there were passing lanes. To round out the story, he arrowed three bucks from the island in three years, including a nine-pointer and an eight-pointer.

From this lesson, I've learned to start with a base map and work my way up to the stereo maps. Then, the final examination is less apt to be a confusing guessing game. Despite all of this, there will be times when you'll just have to go into the field for accurate interpretations. That's what I did for that beaver-pond setup. More often than not, you'll be pleasantly surprised—many areas end up looking even better from the ground than from the air!

Key areas that deer hunters want to identify would be likely bedding areas near food supplies. Besides oaks, look for deer browse in the form of low-growing bushes. In farm country, you want to figure out the "big picture"—travel lanes, woodlot bedding areas, food sources that may also provide cover, drainage ditches and off-road thickets.

Bottlenecks are prime targets for deep-woods hunting and for western tactics. In addition to beaver ponds, strive for topographic constraints such as bluffs, bogs and even open fields. The name of the game, of course, is being in the right place at the right time; the more often deer have to come across your area, the better your chances.

Stereoscopy isn't a tool limited to deer hunters. I have a friend who uses it for locating thick pheasant cover for late-season gunning. He's found some productive pockets that remain hidden from the rank-and-file hunter. And I've stumbled onto some mighty fine grouse coverts while surveying prospective deer country. Next fall, I'm going to wise up and do both grouse and deer reconnaissance with the stereoscope. Then, I'll be able to double up and hunt with the bow in the morning and evening, and with the shotgun at midday—all because of a few photographs and a little instrument.

Stereoscoping Your Buck

Make sure that the glass on the stereoscope is clean. Smudges and fingerprints will cut down on resolution.

Persons with one eye cannot see three dimensionally, but anyone with relatively good vision can successfully use a stereoscope—including eyeglass wearers (be sure to wear them while viewing through the scope). Start by adjusting the scope so

Bowhunter Dean Reidt uses topographic maps to choose likely hotspots on public land. He took this buck, which scored 133⅝ P&Y points, in a crowded wildlife management area by hiking far from roads and other hunters.

that the distance between each lens corresponds to the distance between your eyes. If your pupils aren't located directly over the middle of each lens, you will get dizzy.

Use adequate light, but not too much. Cool light from fluorescent bulbs is best. Also, direct the light from below eye level and from behind the photographs.

Always look straight down through the center of each lens; oblique viewing distorts the model.

To properly identify tree species, knowledge of the topography is essential. Have a topo map for handy reference. A soil map is also helpful because some trees grow only on certain types of soils.

By using shape, color (or shade), texture, size and association with familiar or previously identified objects, vegetation types can be identified. Height easily differentiates shrubs from mature growth. Also, foresters can tell you which tree types are prevalent in a given region.

Evergreens, such as balsam and spruce, are dark (except for hemlock), and their crowns are conical. The pines are more homogeneous, with smaller, rounded crowns. Plantations have a more uniform pattern.

Hardwoods are more difficult to differentiate than evergreens. Aspens have a feathery appearance; oaks are globular, with very large crowns. Apple orchards, like plantations, have a unique pattern.

Time of year affects species identification in aerial photographs. Hardwoods are best discerned with their leaves on; evergreens stand out better in a bare forest.

Scale affects detail. When given an option, choose the smaller scale.

2

Acorns: The Big Buck's Staple

Sometimes, a trophy hunter doesn't have the luxury of taking time to study aerial photos before a hunt. Under these circumstances, knowledge of whitetail foods may be the key to showing him where to begin his big-buck search.

When the computer kicked out a hunting buddy's number for a special muzzleloader hunt held at Fort McCoy, Wisconsin, I put myself in his shoes. His home was a long drive away and he only had one day to scout foreign territory. Where would he start? What would he look for? Since we're both full-time nuts when it comes to hunting whitetails, I was anxious for his report.

Finally he called. In his salutation, the inflection of his voice gave the story away. It was the greatest hunt of his life, he said. There was a super acorn crop, and the place was crawling with whitetails! In one spot, he found so many deer droppings that he had a hard time keeping his footing. He went on to tell about the 20 deer he saw in the white oaks, by noon, and how he had no trouble sneaking up on what proved to be his nicest buck to date.

At first, I was really excited. But after hanging up the phone, I thought about my own experiences with deer and acorns. In all honesty, it sounded more like a fluke than a new way to hunt whitetails. Deer in association with any food source, as a basis for practical hunting strategy, can only be described as an iffy proposition—especially for big bucks. After all, every avid deer

"No food source can offer (deer) as much nutritional value as acorns," said Jim Byford, dean of the School of Agriculture and Home Economics at the University of Tennessee. "You can bet that whenever and wherever acorns become available (deer) will absolutely key in on them to the exclusion of just about everything else."

hunter knows that big bucks don't eat much during the fall.

My prejudices were reinforced the following year when my buddy drew another muzzleloader permit at Fort McCoy. What happened? His acorn connection bombed. The mast crop was way down and because he didn't have any time to scout he ended up wasting precious hours of "The Opener" on the oak ridges, when he should have been down on the bottomlands, where he was very fortunate to kill a young buck eventually.

But since then, I've been forced to rearrange my thinking on how deer foods can affect one's overall hunting success. I've done a flip-flop. I now believe that acorns may indeed hold the key for consistent deer hunting action. I'm not talking just for yearlings and does, but for the real bruisers as well. Unfortunately, it isn't as simple as it might sound. For sure, you have to know a few things about oaks and acorns. More importantly, there are a number of interesting quirks whitetail deer display when it comes to feeding on acorns in the fall. But first the fundamental question: How is it that a food source can aid a hunter in bagging a mature buck, when it's a given that breeding bucks are more interested in sex than food throughout the fall?

The answer comes from Jim Byford, dean of the School of

Bowhunter Mark Pittman took these two eastern Illinois bucks in an area loaded with oaks. A Michigan study finds that deer prefer white oaks to other mast-producing trees.

Agriculture and Home Economics, University of Tennessee at Martin. In completing a radio-tracking study Byford proved conclusively that deer shift their ranges in response to changing food supplies. Further—and here's what hunters ought to know—daily movements "...were very concentrated when food was concentrated, but dispersed when the food supply was dispersed."

Prior to this study, there had been little documentation showing that deer definitely migrate for reasons other than weather. Most of the animals in Byford's study, however, were females. So what about the bucks?

"It's relatively simple," Byford explained. "Bucks are going to be where the does are. No food source can offer as much nutritional value as acorns, and does of breeding age know it. You can bet that whenever and wherever acorns become available, they will absolutely key in on them to the exclusion of just about everything else.''

Now the light bulb should be turned on. Like my buddy says, you'd have to be nuts to ignore anything so significant as to cause a major shift in a deer's range!

This nutty acorn phenomenon is not limited to the South. Jerry P. Duvendeck, a former Michigan Department of Natural Resources biologist, studied deer on acorn diets for three years at the Houghton Lake Wildlife Experiment Station. The results of his work were published in the *Journal of Wildlife Management* in a paper titled, ''The Value of Acorns in the Diet of Michigan Deer.''

Duvendeck was primarily interested in assaying the food value of acorns to see if they could help increase deer survival in years of harsh winters. Control groups of deer, separated in pens, were fed a variety of foods. Included were balsam fir, jack pine, white cedar, oak browse and an acorn supplement consisting of 50 percent Hill's oak, 42 percent northern red oak and eight percent white oak.

Among other things, here's what he found: that deer in captivity, and in the wild, preferred white oak acorns over the others; that only one of the 18 deer involved in the study would not eat all of the acorns, ''shell and all''; that if insect-infested acorns were inadvertently offered, the deer would not eat them; and that deer eating only 1½ pounds of acorns per day per 100 pounds of body weight would easily survive a 90-day winter.

This study is but one example of how finicky deer can be when they decide which acorns to zero in on—a fact that many hunters will sooner or later run up against.

Byford, who is also an avid bowhunter, has noticed a number of equally peculiar feeding traits deer sometimes exhibit. For instance, in years of super abundant mast crops, deer will not only pass up red oak acorns in favor of white oak acorns when both are available in a given area, but they will stick with a specific white oak acorn.

''It's the craziest thing,'' Byford told me during an interview. ''I don't know how they do it, but when acorns are in the process of falling to the ground in heavy-bearing years, most of the deer will only feed on those nuts that have just dropped. I've seen years when the entire countryside was carpeted with acorns, but only

those ridges with fresh-fallen ones attracted deer consistently.''

This is one of the best clues for hunting during years of outstanding mast crops, when patterning deer movements appears to be a game of Russian roulette; trails seem to be leading every which way, and getting a handle on the right entrances and exits is tough.

But how do you tell a "fresh" acorn from one that's been on the ground for awhile? You don't. Instead, says Byford, you let the deer tell you.

"Deer are like most livestock," he said. "When they get up from their beds, they usually defecate. And the beds won't be very far away from the acorn patches they've been working recently. Those areas with the most droppings should definitely be looked at first.

"But that's just the start. Lots of piles of droppings could be misleading. There could be an accumulation from different times when the deer have been in and out of the area, so you have to be able to age the droppings. When you find several ages of droppings in a relatively small area, you can be assured that the deer have been frequenting that particular stand of oaks throughout the fall.''

When Byford says he's sniffing out new deer country, that's exactly what he means—only fresh droppings have a slight odor to them.

Another way to age them is to take the navy bean-shaped pellets apart and examine them. Older ones are more fibrous and dry; fresher ones tend to be moist and pasty.

Once you determine that a particular stand of oaks is being regularly visited by deer, there are two ways to hunt it. One is to look for a primary scrape and figure out the best way to monitor it. Because acorns tend to concentrate does more than any other phenomenon, Byford feels that most, if not all, of a buck's favored scrapes in his home range will be on or very near oak knolls.

Many hunters have never seen a true primary scrape. According to Byford, one of the best places to find one is on the edge of an acorn-studded oak knoll. A hunter-wise buck may be reluctant to venture out into the oak stand, where the underbrush tends to be too thin for comfort. But as the rut approaches, over-anxious bucks will be advertising their presence along the perimeters...and one just might make a foolish daylight excursion into the oaks.

The other method is a tree stand properly placed well back from the major entrance and exit routes. But at which ones?

Generally, the top pick is going to be at a bottleneck between the oaks and the beds. You can look for them at the head of a hollow, near a gap in the ridge or along a natural travel with thick cover that acts as a funnel. But, again, in years of mast abundance, you've got to be flexible and discerning; the deer will be following the acorns as they drop, and last week's hotspot could be worthless this week.

Byford has learned of a clever way to anticipate these changes and keep pace with the deer, rather than reacting to old patterns and forever being one step behind. From years of observation, he has noticed that oaks on the top of a ridge will usually be the first to drop their acorns. Next in line will be those trees that are a little farther down the slope, and so goes the progression. The deer, of course, know this and follow suit. So can you.

What about years when acorns are scarce? That's the easiest hunting of all, because all you have to do is find that rare stand of oaks anointed with deer nuts, and you'll have a hotspot worth a pirate's ransom. Not only will there be a concentration of deer present, but figuring out stand placements at strategic intersection points will be far less perplexing. Locating these hidden treasures is a two-step process.

First, you need to find out where the huntable oak stands are in your region. If you hunt a national forest, contact that agency and ask to talk to one of the foresters. Perhaps he'll have an inventory on file, with some maps to show you. State forests and counties administering tax-forfeited lands also keep such records. And don't forget aerial photographs. Remember that because of their unique crown, oaks are easy to distinguish from other vegetation types.

And second, you should know a little oak biology. There are two kinds of oaks: white oaks and red oaks. Within these two, there are many subspecies, but the main distinguishing feature is that it takes two years for the red oaks to bear fruit; white oaks, on the other hand, are more like an apple tree that flowers, sets and forms its fruit in one growing season. This is an important point, giving any deer hunter the luxury of scouting for red oak acorn production a year in advance—by the first summer, the fruit will be set and can be readily observed on the outer branches.

You should have little difficulty telling the two apart. White oaks have leaves with seven to nine rounded lobes; there are seven to 11 lobes on a red oak leaf and they are sharp, typically being three-pointed.

As mentioned earlier, deer seem to prefer white oaks over red

Author Jeff Murray scored on this big buck because he knew the deer's preferred food was acorns. Studies mentioned in this chapter reveal just how powerful this natural food lure is to a whitetail.

oaks, when given the choice. Also, it should be noted that white oaks dump their acorns first, as early as late August. Thus, it makes a lot of sense to know where both white and red oak stands are, in order to put together an early and late hunting strategy; deer will eventually turn to the red oaks when they've exhausted their supply of white oak acorns.

Oaks prefer moist soils that are well drained. When doing your actual field work take special note of the orientation of each oak grove you find. Mast failures can be the result of a number of factors, but chances are you might be able to isolate them. Then, through a process of elimination, you just might find several areas that could draw deer in like nothing you've ever seen or believed possible.

As an example, if a drought was to blame for this year's mast failure, consider those stands that face north or northeast, where less moisture loss would likely occur. Or, if an early frost hit, consider those stands at higher elevations. Also, red oaks tend to be more susceptible to crop fluctuations than white oaks because they take two years to produce.

To boil it down, I'd look for potential acorn-bearing oaks in this manner: First, note where white oaks might be in relation to red oaks. Then, check out north-facing stands, south-facing stands, higher elevations and lower ones to determine a pattern. Finally, repeat the successful pattern to find the next producing stand or tree. For convenience sake, I'd map this all out on a blown-up topo map or set of aerial photographs. It should prove to be a valuable aid in plotting future hunts centering around acorn crops for years to come.

Incidentally, research completed by Larry Marchinton and Karl Miller, at the University of Georgia, has revealed that in years of mast crop failure bucks may make up to 60 percent less rubs than in years of normal acorn production. (Chapter 3 discusses this in greater detail.) So don't rush to the conclusion that there aren't many good bucks in an area where the mast crop is down from previous years. The bucks may still be present, but their rut intensity "may have been reduced in response to their (physical) condition," Marchinton and Miller reported.

Hunting acorn-related bucks when the rut approaches makes sense, but there is another time when it works on mature bucks. Minnesota bowhunter Myles Keller knows exactly when to do it.

"Apart from the rut, there aren't many percentage opportunities for bowhunters to score on a good buck, especially early in the

If you find only a few rubs in a promising area, don't scratch that area off your "potential" list. Research at the University of Georgia shows that bucks may make 60 percent less rubs during an acorn crop failure.

season," he said. "Hunting around acorns right as they drop, though, is one of the few patterns that is worth a try. For a very limited time, even smart bucks in the 4½- to 5½-year-old range will load up on acorns. But you have to catch them coming out real early in the morning, or you'll blow your chance there until the rut."

By "real early," Keller, who is profiled in Chapter 10, advocates being on your stand at least two hours before sunrise (be sure to check with local game regulations). There is just no other way. And this pattern only lasts for a short time before the mating urge takes over and hunger becomes nothing more than a minor nuisance for several months to come.

To pull this early-season trick off, you have to have a good mast crop that's dropping by the bow season opener. That usually means white oaks will be involved, which, as mentioned, tend to drop their acorns earlier than most other species. This time, though, you'll be setting up on the edges, hoping to catch a buck coming off a late night snack.

Now you know the score on deer nuts. The next time a whitetail authority chooses to disagree with you, don't be intimidated. Consider the mighty oaks: at one time they were just a bunch of nuts.

3

Rub Your Buck
The Right Way

So after carefully studying topo maps and aerial photos and further homing in on a likely looking trophy buck lair, it's time to narrow your intended hunting area even more. Now it's time to answer every hunter's question: Just where does a trophy buck spend most of his time during the deer season?

Revolutionary new scientific research indicates that there is one bit of whitetail truth that is really worth seeking. It's so important, according to researchers, that it can affect the exact timing of the rut each fall; it can foretell if a particular section of woods is dominated by mature bucks or is inhabited by yearlings; it can reveal to you exactly where a big buck is hiding out, both before the rut and during it; and it can even tell you exactly where to find the most dominant buck in any given area.

Of all the deer sign hunters snoop around for, which one is it? It is the one that gets us excited the most, but probably affects our personal hunting strategy the least.

Rubs!

Indeed, an antler rub is much like the weather: everyone talks about it but nobody does anything about it. But how can this be? For years, biologists and trophy hunters have led us to the conclusion that rubs are of secondary importance—that hot scrapes and other fresh sign is where it's at. Besides, a rub is only evidence that a buck once passed by a certain spot, and certainly not a clue as to where he's likely to be in the future, right? Ah, not necessarily so. At least one wildlife manager who hunts trophy bucks with the same intensity he seeks out new research data advocates positioning a tree stand within shooting distance of a particular rubbed tree!

But I'm getting ahead of myself. First, because the knowledge of buck rubs is pretty common fodder amongst most hunters, it would be a good idea to update ourselves with some of the latest findings. Much of it conflicts with suppositions from the 1960s and 1970s, and could thus lead to a better understanding of the role buck rubs play in deer society—and how the astute hunter may capitalize on it.

Originally, rubs were thought to be a method bucks used to remove the velvet from their antlers. Then, popular whitetail lore held that rubs were territorial markers, helping to establish the home range of breeding bucks. Today, most whitetail authorities agree to disagree on both points. Still, the exact purpose of rubs remains a mystery. Mounting evidence, however, indicates that rubs are far more significant than early research suggested, and that they are part of a complex communication system *within* the sexes, as well as *between* them. These signposts are more than a display of dominance. As more light is being shed on this intriguing subject, a major breakthrough for biologists—and hunters— appears to be on the horizon in the near future.

The most far-reaching theory, with a convincing amount of evidence to support it, was presented at a symposium in Poland by University of Georgia researchers Larry Marchinton, W. Matt Knox and Karl Miller. Their fascinating paper (''Whitetailed Deer Signposts and Their Role as a Source of Priming Pheromones'') referenced a number of recent works, including two the authors had published in the *Journal of Wildlife Management*, and in the *Journal of Mammology*.

In essence, the paper's controversial position is that whitetail signposts in a specific geographic region play an important role in determining the ultimate timing of nearby does' estrus cycles. Because the timing of the rut is dependent upon when does first go into heat, this information could be very helpful to deer hunters. Wouldn't it be nice to know, for example, that one could tell if the peak of the rut was going to be early, late, or ''on time'' during a particular hunting season by merely examining buck rubs in a given locale?

''There is a broad time period,'' Karl Miller told me, ''that can

For years, biologists and trophy hunters suggested that rubs were of secondary importance—that hot scrapes and other fresh sign were the important items. However, revolutionary new scientific research indicates that hunters have been overlooking one of the most important big buck signs.

be fine-tuned locally, ahead or backwards, significantly.''

How does it all work? The key could be priming pheromones—agents that do not necessarily cause a behavioral action or reaction (as do sex pheromones), but a biological change nonetheless—that are deposited through antler rubbing. In this case, these pheromones act as a biostimulant that induces early ovulation. In a related study, published in the *Journal of Wildlife Management*, authors Louis Verme and John Ozoga came up with the same conclusion: Michigan pen-raised does, observed in close proximity with bucks, bred earlier in the breeding season than those outside the pens.

But what about deer in the wild and those in other regions of the nation? The same thing can be expected to occur—the more buck rubs in a given area, the more likely an early estrus will take place among the does. The Mt. Holly Plantation in South Carolina is a good case in point. A five-year study was conducted by Guynn, Sweeney and Hamilton. Conception dates were analyzed at the beginning and end of the study period. Also, the herd was managed during that time by various hunting regulations so that a more balanced population would result in a better buck-to-doe ratio.

The results concur with the Michigan study. In one year, the peak of the rut as evidenced by the mean conception date proved to be November 11. Later, when there were more bucks and more older bucks, proportionately, the mean conception date was October 23. And the range (the length of the breeding season), during the study period, decreased from 96 to 59 days. (It is important to note that deer in the South enjoy an extended growing season, and are not forced to complete their mating ritual in time for an adequate gestation period. Weather constraints upon deer in the North decrease the range of conception dates considerably.)

This new information on timing the rut could end a lot of frustration many hunters must deal with each fall as they attempt to schedule vacation time to coincide with traditional rut dates for their state. In the past, I've seen conflicting evidence about when the rut is supposed to peak in my home state of Minnesota to the point that no date seems reliable. I've noticed years when the bucks seemed most vulnerable in early November, and years when late November was best—in spite of the traditional November 12-18 peak date predicted by officials at the Minnesota Department of Natural Resources.

But just how do you go about predicting the rut? Larry

A South Carolina study suggests that you can judge buck density by the number of rubs, like the one this bowhunter has found, in an area. Of course, a single buck will make more than one rub. The Mt. Holly Plantation research, discussed in this chapter, looks deeper into what rubs really tell you as a hunter.

Marchinton, one of the nation's most respected whitetail researchers, doesn't claim to have any pat answers. But he does have a hunch:

"I'd hunt—and I mean hunt—for normal buck sign that might indicate a good buck population is present in my deer country," he said. "And not in general terms, but for a specific home range. Then, I'd probably look real hard at the traditional rut date state officials give to see how reliable it has been in the past. There may be a basis for some back-dating to get the 'real' peak (period)."

How much to back-date would likely be a variable that is influenced by latitude. In the North, as mentioned earlier, deer have a shorter growing season and must get on with the business of procreation. A week might be appropriate. As one goes farther south, more days could probably be subtracted; in the South Carolina study previously mentioned, the mean peak of the rut advanced by nearly three weeks when more bucks were present.

This should give you the absolute peak of the rut, but you wouldn't necessarily want to "x" those dates on the calendar—most of the mature bucks will probably be tending hot does by night and resting up during the day, and their mating urge will likely be satisfied. Or the opposite could occur: A particular buck you've been patterning may have gone off the deep end, chasing does into the next county. But a week or two on either side of your new peak rut date could be another matter. That might prove to be *the* time to be in the woods. Bucks should be on the prowl in more predictable patterns, looking for that occasional, receptive doe.

What if your field reconnaissance shows that there are fewer bucks in one particular area than another? That might be a good time to stick closer to the traditional rut period established by state biologists. There, the does may have had less exposure to rubs in the woods, and biostimulation may not have occurred to the same degree as in other places. With these deer "on schedule," the flexible hunter might enjoy additional pre-rut and post-rut peaks by simply hunting different areas.

Besides aiding you in timing the rut locally, buck rubs can give you a fairly accurate forecast of buck density in a given herd. If you put two and two together, you'll see that the Mt. Holly Plantation study indicated that there were more bucks in the population toward the end, which led to more buck rubs, which led to the biostimulation of female deer. So do more rubs mean more bucks? Perhaps. More importantly, more good-sized rubs, partic-

"When your scouting notes turn up a lot of early rubs, there's a good chance that the age structure of the deer herd is an older one," deer biologist Larry Marchinton reported.

ularly later on in the season, could mean more dominant bucks in the region. But it isn't quite that simple. And this is why deer hunters—especially trophy hunters—ought to pay strict attention to both the size and timing of every buck rub they see in the woods.

The small-rub/small-buck, big-rub/big-buck theory has been touted by everyone for years. Although it holds some water, it has been oversimplified and overstated. During a recent two-year study on rubs, Larry Marchinton and Karl Miller located and measured 529 rubs in five study areas. Their conclusion? No significant difference in rub sizes was found between areas with different age structures; rubs in yearling-dominated habitats were almost the same general size as those where two out of three bucks were older than a year and a half. A further breakdown of this long-held theory especially occurs in early fall. That's when most of the rubs will be made on bushes and smaller trees—and by dominant bucks.

"They look more like thrashings than the larger, sign post rub you see later on in the season," Marchinton told me. "The significance of these early-season rubs is pretty straightforward: Younger bucks don't make many. So when your scouting notes turn up a lot of early rubs, there's a good chance that the age structure of the deer herd is an older one."

Finding early-season rubs may be the tip-off to a good buck, but locating rubs at this time of the year is not going to be as easy as you might think. Unlike sign post rubs, which are typically found on larger-diameter trees in more open territory, a buck's first rubs of the fall are invariably going to be in thicker underbrush. And this is another valuable clue that could translate into practical hunter strategy. I found out just how significant this phenomenon is when Noble Carlson—a trophy buck tracker discussed in more detail in Chapter 15—finally revealed to me how he narrows down the areas he will eventually hunt when the snow flies.

"Look, I've got less than five deer to the square mile to work with in my part of the country," he snapped after I had been pestering him on how he looks for big-buck areas. "With these numbers, I better find a way to boil it down. The best way I know of is with rubs. Of course, you've got to have a good feel for the kind of country big bucks tend to hang out in, but it's those September rubs that tell me where to look later on."

Then he told me something that really caught my attention: He especially looks for spots with early rubs clumped in close proximity to one another, often found in a semi-circle. That is usually going to be the very center of a big buck's core area and

Finding early-season rubs may be the tip-off to a good buck, but locating rubs at this time of the year won't be easy. A buck's first rubs of the fall will be in thick underbrush, not on the larger-diameter trees typical of late-season rubs.

close to his preferred bedding site(s). Although Noble doesn't bowhunt he knows where he can expect to find the largest set of tracks come firearms season.

Think of the implications! Once you know where a buck beds in his core area, the rest of the scouting game is a cinch. Naturally, you'll be very careful about how you'll set up near it—certainly not within it—and you'll take your time figuring out entrances, exits, thermal currents and wind direction.

As you do this, keep in mind that these pre-rut rubs must be identified early. If you limit most of your scouting to when the leaves have dropped, they could be mistaken for rubs made later on by lesser bucks, because both types are usually not gouged out on larger trees. And after a recent rain, it's tough to tell fresh rubs from those made a month or so earlier.

What if you find an abundance of rubs in September, but they seem to be scattered throughout the region? Is that the work of several smaller bucks? Not according to John Ozoga, who has worked since 1964 with deer in a one-mile enclosure at the Cusino Wildlife Research Station in Upper Michigan.

"Where you have a lot of mature bucks," he told me, "you'll see rubbing activity early in the fall. But in areas where hunter pressure is extremely high with few dominant bucks, you will see a lot of 'delayed rubbing' by yearlings, and you may not see any rubs until October."

This all translates into some mighty good news: You can't come home empty-handed from a September scouting session when rubs are your target. If you see few rubs after a diligent search, you can bet that there probably aren't many, if any, dominant bucks in the area. The lone exception would be a mast crop failure which, as mentioned in the previous chapter, tends to reduce buck rubbing. And if you find plenty of rubs in different areas, you should have several nice bucks to go after. Best of all, if your scouting notes turn up lots of rubs concentrated near thick cover, beds and lots of droppings, you might have hit the jackpot.

How many rubs is a lot? Marchinton and Miller came up with some interesting figures. From their computations they discovered that, on the average, a typical buck in their study made anywhere from 69 to 538 rubs in one year, with the average being 300. And during the peak rubbing period, 15 to 20 rubs—or more—were probably made per day! Later on in the fall, when dominant bucks approach the fever and frenzy of the rutting season, their rubs will take on a completely different look. Larger, more aromatic

This bowhunter has found an important rub that scientists are just beginning to understand. Scientists say that a rub like this on a good-sized tree is usually made by the area's dominant buck. Studies show that it will be revisited by the dominant buck year after year, as well as during the season. Also, scientists have discovered that three or four other bucks will use this same sign post.

trees—cedar, sumac, hemlock, pines, black cherry—will be the target, and these rubs will stand out like a traffic cop on a main street. Also, the more dominant a buck is, the more scarred trees there will be in his rutting territory. As Ozoga says, "The buck is saying 'Here I am, I'm number one,' and he'll advertise that slogan plenty; lesser bucks simply have less to say and say it less."

Finally, a specific type of rub has been uncovered recently that is generating as much excitement in some circles as the scrape studies did back in the early 1970s. Dr. James C. Kroll, director of the Institute for Whitetail Deer Management & Research at Stephen F. Austin University in Nacogdoches, Texas, is credited with its discovery and is its chief authority.

"I first noticed these rubs a few years ago on islands in swamps and along the edges where the bucks would bed," he told me. "They tend to be very large—my biggest to date was made on an 11-inch cedar. But what makes them unique, is the fact that they are *revisited* by a dominant buck year after year, as well as *during the season*. And recently, I have discovered that up to three or four bucks will use the same sign post."

Kroll is quick to point out that you can't expect to find these markers just anywhere. Typically, one is found on a cedar tree, which is "the only tree able to stand up to that kind of repeated abuse," he said. Also, they show up in deer herds that are managed for trophy potential, so you have "the makings of a territoriality-type behavior among several dominant bucks."

Kroll doesn't know why dominant bucks revisit these sign-posts, but he feels they are like a signature. He witnessed several bucks last year working over the same tree and he even managed to record it on video. "Each deer is very slow and deliberate with his tines," he told me. "And they are careful to lick it repeatedly and rub their foreheads across it. You definitely get the feeling that something important is communicated."

It's exciting to keep up with the latest research on whitetails. Old theories fall and new ones replace them at an alarming pace these days. That's both fun and frustrating. But the real rub, in light of the above discoveries, is that we may have overlooked something of great value in our quest for truth.

4

Places Without Faces

R eading maps, locating food sources and scouting for rubs are all good ways to begin that trophy search. But harvesting a true bruiser oftentimes involves going one step further than the next guy, or discovering a clue that he has overlooked.

There's an old deer camp adage that says "You can't eat deer sign." What it means, of course, is that you've got to see deer to score. It sounds simple, but if today's hunter is going to take a good buck, he has to look in some offbeat places. There's a ton of competition in areas where hunters abound, and the deer there wise up quickly. Spikes, forkhorns and the occasional rack buck will fall to the crowds, but to score consistently on a trophy buck is an entirely different matter.

Over the years, I've discovered five honest-to-goodness hotspots where you'll see more deer than hunters. Guaranteed. And you won't have to travel great distances to find them—in fact, they may be in your own backyard, where you've driven by them for years. Not necessarily in order of importance or frequency, they are: swamp islands, river routes, highway corridors, pockets of private holdings amidst large public tracts and small public tracts surrounded by large private holdings.

Each is unique, but they all share two characteristics: They concentrate deer, and they are generally avoided by hunters. To fully appreciate this precious union, let's go back to last fall.

Despite our increasingly urbanized society, it is possible for bucks like this to find an area where they can avoid hunter pressure. This chapter shows you how to find such a big buck spot.

Chances are good that you, like most serious deer hunters, did your homework in the field well before the season opened. Deer sign—primarily trails, beds, rubs and scrapes—were noted and carefully evaluated; soon a pattern or two emerged. Then you built or selected your stand and, for better or worse, stood your ground for that season.

If you were lucky, the deer continued in their daily habits and you had your moment of truth. Just as often, however, those patterns became interrupted and the buck never materialized.

Why? Every circumstance is slightly different, but the interrupting agent is usually the same culprit—another hunter. So the end result of all your diligent scouting and scheming is the selection of an area where deer will either spend their evenings or, more likely, an area where they used to be.

That situation leaves only two options: Take hunter pressure into account or totally avoid it. The former is risky business, unless you are intimately familiar with a given geographic area, as well as with the deer and the hunters who occupy it. Even then, there are variables to contend with, such as new faces or old ones doing different things.

On the other hand, what if another hunter never entered your area? At the very least, pre-season scouting could tell you where you could expect to see deer later on during the season. That's the exciting thing about finding places without faces.

But is it really practical for the average hunter in an increasingly urbanized society to totally avoid hunter pressure? At first, I thought the concept was limited in application only to those states with lots of public land and widely scattered population centers. Lately, I've come to realize that the solution is far from simply putting distance between myself and the nearest road. Deep woods deer, with their enigmatic movement patterns and thin numbers, can make for tough hunting conditions. So I'm not out to get lost but, rather, I'm looking to make a find: a particular patch of real estate where I know I'm going to see a deer and no people.

Finding that spot boils down to understanding a little bit about human nature and wildlife behavior.

Take the first area, a swamp island. I'll never forget the day I made that discovery. It was during a special refuge hunt when game managers opened certain sections of the refuge to the hunting public because deer populations had reached explosive levels. The previous year had provided some fabulous results, with a very high success rate and many good bucks registered, and apparently, the

Craig Cousins with one of his many Wisconsin whitetails from places without faces.

word had gotten out. Consequently, I spent more time just looking for some cover that lacked red or Blaze Orange jackets.

In the process, I bumped into an old-timer who was dragging a 10-point buck through the woods. He wore a fatigued face and he was drenched with sweat, so I offered him a hand in getting his trophy back to his pickup.

After we arrived at the truck, he thanked me and as he was about to leave, he gave me a strange look.

"I owe you one," he said in a raspy voice. "If you can keep a secret, I'll show you where I got that buck. There's more where he came from."

"You don't have to do that," I responded. Then I began to hedge a bit. "Did you really see other bucks besides that big one?"

"Are you kidding?" he snapped. "I let a bunch of scrawny spikes and forkhorns go by—and a six-pointer."

It took us only 45 minutes to get to the spot; it would have taken even less time, but the tag alder thickets made for slow going. The old man had found a real gold mine all right. Those deer had a perfect fortress that was well-buttressed on all sides. It was a small knoll surrounded by a tangled alder swamp. The knoll couldn't have been more than three acres.

Swamp islands often serve many needs of a buck: a reprieve from four and two-legged predators; solitude, which seems to be a socially ingrained preference among mature bucks in a given environment; food and shelter from the elements; and a good bedding and breeding site. And remember, these little patches are often the only places where a deer can avoid standing in water without traveling great distances. Thus, they can be a natural attractor of big game from that standpoint alone.

Prospects are good that you'll find a number of swamp islands to choose from locally. Just purchase the proper quadrangle contour map of your area, and look up the marsh symbol. A potential knoll will reveal itself as an isolated ring, or doughnut, in a sea of marsh symbols.

Next, narrow down the prospects further by studying the area(s) with a stereoscope and a set of aerial photographs.

The final step is to take these swamp stands at "face value" to make sure that bucks are using them and hunters aren't. I do this by covering them during the deer season, looking for human tracks as well as buck tracks. I want to be certain that I'll have the spot all to myself. Then, the following summer, I'll set up my ambush by choosing my stand and cutting sight lines well in advance of the season. Each year, I keep on the lookout for new areas to consider for the following year.

Since I first learned about this hotspot, when the old man brought me to his coveted little knoll, I've found enough new ones to convince me that this pattern is reliable and repeats itself wherever whitetails and swamps can be found. Not all produce, but those that do will yield venison for years to come.

A brother to the swamp island—and just as productive in certain situations—is an island splitting a river, or one that's close to the mainland of a lake or pothole. Wounded deer often seek out these areas when hotly pursued—a point worth remembering should the situation arise.

If hunting swamp islands sounds too rigorous, in spite of the

A small knoll buttressed on all sides by a tangled alder swamp can be the perfect big buck hotspot. On a topographic map, such a knoll will appear as an isolated ring, or doughnut, in a sea of marsh symbols.

If you hunt canoe routes, be forewarned that deer are excellent swimmers and not the least bit intimidated by water. Also, pressured bucks will often evade their predators by taking to the water and masking their scent.

prospects of seeing more deer than hunters, there's another untapped area with easy travel available: canoe routes. This is evidence of yet another hunter neurosis. For some reason, some hunters just don't or won't engage in certain activities: Duck hunters don't like to portage, pheasant gunners won't camp out and deer hunters are gun-shy of canoes.

With the advent of a plethora of canoe routes being charted and mapped across the country (due, in part, to legislation such as the Wild and Scenic Rivers Act), finding a canoe route with miles of decent whitetail habitat all to yourself is entirely possible. Begin your search with your local DNR agency, then contact chambers of commerce in areas with a river or two (some may promote only summer tubing, so be alert) and local canoe clubs.

Your chief concern is a relatively accurate map showing put-ins and take-outs, rapids, dams and campsites carefully marked to scale. Employing two cars—one parked at the take-out point before putting-in—will save on backtracking upstream, giving you more time to hunt.

Canoes allow effortless and silent travel, as well as versatility. Don't like the deer sign along one stretch? Paddle downstream until you find fresher sign. And don't be caught off guard by deer working the riverbed right along the banks.

Rivers are also a natural in providing good deer habitat for a number of reasons. Vegetation is usually denser and lusher along bottomland, yielding both feed and cover for game, water is obviously available in abundance. Deer are excellent swimmers and not the least bit intimidated by white water. And deer like to evade their enemies by doubling back on their trail and losing their scent in the river—a ploy often used by pressured bucks.

Waterways can also provide "easy" hunting because game trails often parallel the contours of the river banks, providing good tracking and easy walking. Noise is also muffled by gurgling water, so you can step on more than your allotment of twigs and probably get away with it.

Swamp islands and river routes work for the enterprising hunter because there is a basic weakness in the mettle of many modern hunters: They take the paths of least resistance, involving the least amount of hassle. That's easy to understand, but there's another psychological trap that manifests itself among the hunting community that defies definition. For lack of a better term, I call it the Farthest Armchair Route (FAR) syndrome.

This malady can be used to the advantage of any deer hunter once the condition is properly diagnosed. It usually goes something like this: We head out the door and drive the highway to a country road, turn on to that road, keep turning, take another fork, take the dirt road, swing off onto the forest road and then to the foot trail. The major point is that we keep looking for lesser traveled roads, staying in the car or truck as long as we can. In the process, however, we pass up bucks...especially along the highway.

I have a friend who is a game warden, and one of his least favorite tasks is tending to road kills.

"I wish hunters would throw away all those crazy manuals," he said out of the blue one fall day.

"What manuals?" I asked.

"The ones that say that the best hunting is found along dirt roads," he replied.

He did raise an interesting point. What about road kills? We all know the keen interest that various states take in lowering traffic fatalities. One of the tedious records that they keep is the location of all reported car/deer collisions. With a short letter, any hunter can shortcut a lot of field work by requesting such information in a given area. The agency to contact is usually the state transportation or highway department.

Lands adjacent to major highways are good bets, not only because of the FAR syndrome, but also because highways are a natural barrier that somewhat constrict daytime movement of deer. Again, topographic maps can further refine and pinpoint a local hotspot.

A neighbor of my butcher used to bring in a bragging-size buck for processing each fall for many years. The only information about his hotspot that I could get out of him was the name of the nearest city and the fact that he could "hear car tires" from his stand. When I found out that he switched cars with his uncle during the deer season, I knew what to look for, and a year later I saw it: a blue pickup parked off the right-of-way of the highway that leads out of town.

When I confronted him, he admitted that there was "a certain area that deer traveled parallel to a certain highway because of a certain creekbed that meandered nearby." He found the area by checking a topo map after he narrowly missed hitting a big buck with his car on the highway one Halloween night. He saw a grand total of two people in those woods during a 10-year period, and one of them was looking for a lost hubcap.

The many warning signs posted along highways, alerting motorists to deer crossings, can also be an indication of roadside deer concentrations. They aren't put up without reason, so pay attention to their locations next time you're driving through deer country on a major thoroughfare.

Perhaps the best antidote for the FAR syndrome is a conversation with frequent highway travelers—truckers, salesmen or highway patrolmen—followed up by a stroll along suggested corridors during the deer season. You'll be amazed at what you've been passing up.

The best opening-day stand that I've ever seen, bar none, belongs to a friend of mine named John who lives and hunts in Ohio. At first glance (and probably at second and third), the little

For some reason, duck hunters don't like to portage, pheasant gunners won't camp out and deer hunters shy from canoes. But often, canoes can provide you with access to productive places without faces.

wooded fence row looks like a good hunting spot for cottontails, maybe, but certainly not for bucks—especially the huge ones that my friend bags almost every year. And the setup is common across North America where private farms are scattered within transitional woodlands.

Wherever you find national, state or county forests near small tracts of cultivated fields, you've found great potential for a similar surprise attack. On the forest lands, deer invariably get pressured—often from all sides—toward creek bottoms, swales and isolated woodlots on nearby private holdings. All you have to do is determine the most likely routes that bucks will take from the forest to the farmland, and obtain permission in advance.

For the most part, bucks will take the most direct route available where cover can break up their outline against otherwise open fields. Brushy fence rows are ideal.

"I felt downright silly when I first set up at the 'T' of two fence lines," John confessed to me. "I thought that no self-respecting buck would expose himself in this dangerous bottle-neck."

But John stuck it out for a whole 20 minutes and had his mind changed in a hurry.

"It sounded like World War III over in the woods as soon as the sun came up," he said. "Then, all of a sudden, this big buck just popped out of nowhere, heading right for me. It was as easy a shot as a guy could ask for."

Two more things stand out about his spot. First, the farmer, who doesn't hunt, was glad to have John help him out by thinning crop-eating deer that "trespassed" on his farm. Second, John always sees big bucks—no spikes or forkhorns—in areas like that. But I guess that's OK.

The final hotspot is one that's especially common to the Midwest, in states like Kansas, Nebraska, Iowa and the Dakotas, and it's not *under*-hunted...it's *un*hunted! I learned firsthand about these areas while pheasant hunting more than 10 years ago.

Scattered across the nation's midriff in prime pheasant habitat is a myriad of state and federal tracts that are managed for wildlife, ostensibly waterfowl and upland birds. Wildlife Management Areas (WMAs) and public shooting grounds also provide the perfect sanctuary for pressured bucks in midseason.

As a bowhunter, it was easy to settle into a WMA and wait for bird hunters to push through the tangled thatches and swamp

If you're a bowhunter, settle into a Wildlife Management Area and wait for bird hunters to push through the tangled thatches and swamp thickets. Eventually, deer like this one will be driven from their beds.

thickets. Eventually, deer would be driven toward me along fairly predictable travel lanes.

Lately, however, I've found that WMAs, especially the smaller ones, can conceal a mighty fine buck.

While pheasant hunting one fall, I found a large set of deer tracks that led into a half-acre swale that was part of just such a public tract, but it was bisected from the rest of the area by a ditch bank.

I walked the entire perimeter of that patch, and I knew that any deer within must have winded me. I entered the swale. Suddenly, no more than 10 feet away, a heavy-necked, wide-racked buck sprung to his feet as if he had been bedded on a trampoline. I must have been the first hunter to have passed that buck in a long time. Apparently, even other pheasant hunters considered the patch unworthy of a going over.

That was one startled buck, and I was one surprised rooster hunter. But in hindsight, I should have known that it was another one of those places without faces that deer seek out and that deer hunters avoid. Next time, I won't be so surprised.

5

Bucks On
The Back 40

But places without faces aren't the only homes of trophy whitetail bucks. Some of the other areas harboring the big boys are a little more obvious than that. Take farm country, for example.

You don't have to look far to see how big whitetails grow in farm country. In one year a new No. 2 and a new No. 3 Pope & Young buck, scoring 201⅛ and 197⅝ from Ohio and Minnesota, respectively, were taken by bowhunters from farm country. I'd bet my last broadhead that the new No. 1 whitetail is going to be taken by a bowhunter and that he'll take it close to someone's plowed fields.

But not everyone who hunts farmland sees it this way. For many, it's a frustrating experience comprised mostly of long shots under low-light conditions. The good bucks they do see are usually in distant fields, feeding at night. Very few hunters end up with close shots during the day. Why? I think it's a simple matter of hunting farm country deer all wrong, or at least partly wrong. Sure, there's more than one way to skin a cat, and there are plenty of ways to kill a buck. When it comes to trophy whitetails on the farm, however, there's a particular formula I have learned that is second to none. And I'm not talking about deer drives, either. My mentor, noted bowhunter Myles Keller, is the principal author of the system, and his record speaks for itself. Myles is closing in on

Bowhunter Gene Lengsfeld took this record-book buck in farm country.

two dozen Pope & Young entries in the record book.

The heart of the system is the very opposite approach than most modern deer hunters take. Keller doesn't merely put in time at predetermined areas (naturally based on scouting forays) and hope for the best. That method is bound to tip off your presence to the deer in the area no matter how careful you are about controlling your scent, noise and movement. And by the time the peak activity of the bigger bucks hits, most hunters, especially bowhunters, are suffering from burnout. The net effect is a hunter who is not really sharp, and who is simply going through the motions. This scenario, Keller believes, repeats itself each fall for at least 90 percent of the country's hunters.

"Once a big buck knows he's being hunted," Keller insists, "he turns into an entirely different animal. He's almost a separate species when compared to lesser bucks and others who haven't been pressured."

So how do you get yourself on even terms with an "unalarmed" buck? How do you learn his backyard without polluting it with your scent? And how in the world can you pattern a mature deer in order to be in the right place at the right time?

One key is not to overhunt. It's just not a percentage shot to be

Here is another big farm-country buck, this one taken by Curt Van Lith. This typical buck is the largest ever taken in Minnesota by a bowhunter.

waiting for bucks to come by when they're not active. And you can rule out stalking in most farm country, except for limited situations involving deer in corn patches. But it's the hunting season, you say, and who can sit around waiting for the rut? Well, you don't have to. Time will be on your side only if you use it wisely.

Here is an outline of the system that has been the downfall of many a fine buck.

Plan to spend the first three or four days of the season hunting hard, not scouting. Your scouting should have been done prior to the season, beginning with the previous spring or, better yet, late winter. You should have a good idea of the general areas deer are working. Bedding areas near water can be good. So are trails leading to fields.

The main advantage of the early part of the season is the fact that the deer haven't been pursued for many months. Granted, the bugs bother the deer, and the bucks have a hard time in the heat with their heavy coats. But they won't be using their senses to avoid people. In farmland, deer are somewhat used to human scent and human activity, and they are approachable...until, that is, they sense danger. Unfortunately, this early honeymoon period typically lasts no more than two or three days in most parts of the country. Then, mature bucks become strictly nocturnal.

The next step is to put the bow or gun away and get out the binoculars. Glassing farm country is the single most important aspect of patterning deer, and anyone who hasn't learned this vital lesson is handicapping himself. Many hunters own a pair of the old standard 8 x 30s, or the newer 8 x 20 wide angle, pocket field glasses. But a more powerful unit is better. Last year I graduated to a set of Nikon 7 x 50s (7.3 degrees), and it was well worth the expenditure. Not only is the resolution sharper and the magnification greater, but the light gathering capabilities are superior—a definite plus for glassing early morning and early evening critters at long distances.

You can save a lot of time by getting leads on where to glass, instead of starting from scratch. The mailman, propane gas deliverer or the farmer himself are prime sources of information. Because these individuals spend more time in a given area *on a routine basis*, they not only can tell you about favored deer crossing areas, but which ones are currently being used.

Once you get a tip or a personal sighting of a worthy buck the next step is to glass the area in which he is associated. You'll find definite patterns that tend to repeat themselves, and eventually a

Squirrels and birds will pick kernels from a corn cob, like this hunter discovered. Deer, meanwhile, will bite into the cob and will probably leave teeth marks.

weak link in the buck's overall routine might emerge. But don't expect it to leap out at you from one or two glassing sessions. It usually takes several weeks.

What should be your focal points, and what weaknesses might you discover? The first observation should be how deer use and react to varying wind conditions. In the openness of farm country, big bucks that are hunted hard rarely venture out during daylight without a favoring wind. It may sound elementary, but when you do find a particular area that seems to be inhabited more frequently than others by a good buck, you'll quickly see how impenetrable his lair is; no matter how you try to enter it, he'll likely scent you or see you. But this can be overcome.

Your next task—and this is a controversial concept, one that is a no-no in most hunting circles today—is to zero in on the major bedding areas of the does in a local social group. We're not talking about beds on the edges of food sources, but main, or preferred, bedding areas that offer both comfort and safety to the does: shade from the sun, shelter from adverse winds, strategic location for scenting oncoming danger, etc. These areas stand out from occasional bedding areas by the intensity of sign. You will notice, for instance, more droppings here than anywhere, and the beds will always seem fresh. Also, you will find lots of rubs downwind from these beds. This then becomes the key to unlocking the mystery of knowing exactly where to place your stand.

Yes, you move in and actually hunt the bedding area. Like I said, this approach has been considered taboo by many experts for a long time. It's not without good reason. It is so easy to be detected by several animals, compared to just one, because you're dealing with dozens of eyes, ears and noses instead of two. And once your presence is detected in the bedding area, you've just blown all future chances for penetrating that family circle there for the rest of the deer season. That's why most experts don't risk it. They prefer to hunt scrapes, trails connecting bedding and feeding areas and escape routes, because they know they're not putting all their eggs in one basket, so to speak.

But Keller has me convinced that his approach is the closest thing to a sure bet that you're ever going to find for trophy bucks in farm country. That is, *if* you do everything right. Now that's a mighty big "if," but things can be done right by anyone who is willing to pay the price.

OK, let's say you've found the main bedding area. Now what? From my experiences, it's easier to tell you how not to hunt it than

Missourian Chuck Myers consistently takes big bucks like this one near farm country.

how to do it successfully. For example, the one thing you don't want to do is spend any unnecessary time there. That means no pruning or cutting—no walking around whatsoever. And for heaven's sake, do not exit the area in the direction the deer might be feeding at night. Again, these precautions might seem rudimentary, but nine bowhunters out of 10 walk the fields (where deer feed), instead of the woodlots, after dark. Perhaps you're beginning to get a feel for how picky you have to be to make a perfect setup in the main bedding area.

Now you're ready to choose the perfect place for your stand. You want to get up as high as you dare, possibly sacrificing optimum arrow placement for controlling your scent. Of course, that means you will have to limit your shots to about 20 yards.

Remember all those buck rubs you saw downwind from the beds? That's where the big boys will be chomping at the bit, waiting for the first does to go into heat. So during the pre-rut phase, before a majority of the does go into heat, your best bet is to let the occasional older doe (that goes into estrus a month early) draw in your buck. This means that your ambush site should be located downwind from the does' bedroom, close to where the buck(s) will be waiting impatiently.

Once that stand goes up, you're ready to shift into first gear and get the bow out. But you don't hunt this stand. Not just yet. Instead, pick a fenceline close by, one that lets you monitor the general area, so as to reveal what Keller refers to as "the big picture." Hunt the fenceline hard, but don't necessarily expect it to produce your buck. It might. But don't count on it. It will, however, tell you when it's time to go into the bedroom. When you see minor rutting activity—nervous does running from bucks, or excited bucks making new rubs—it's time to move in.

By now you're probably as much on edge as the bucks; you've waited long enough. Most of your buddies have been hunting a solid month, while you've been spending valuable vacation time laying in the weeds. But now it's your time.

As you enter your stand under the cloak of total darkness, you must be prepared to stay there for the entire day. You simply cannot afford to weasel out for greener pastures if you don't get any action right away. Your leaving could well ruin it for the remainder of the season. Armed with this frame of mind, you should also have everything you need to stick it out for 12 hours: a urine bottle, proper clothing and food for a quiet lunch.

If nothing materializes, do not return to the stand on successive

Some hunters think that big bucks have a sixth sense about danger. Bowhunter Myles Keller says that if you pollute an area with your scent, other animals will avoid it. "Then what you've got is a pocket, or vacuum with no natural scent to it. Bucks seem to pick up on this without any problem."

mornings. Too much traffic will be felt by the deer. Instead, come back in a few days fully prepared to repeat the vigil. Also, if you spook any animals on the way in, strongly consider backing out for another day. And if you oversleep, don't even attempt it.

To ensure continued animal traffic Keller establishes ''scent posts'' near his tree stand with a product that remained a secret until a hunting companion pressed him to market it. "The idea behind 'Keller's Killer' is to create several scent posts in the immediate area," Keller told me. "It's a urine-based product that arouses the curiosity of wild animals and plays on their instincts. What happens is that after you apply some to a rock or stump, animals will stop by, investigate and urinate directly over your deposit. Sometimes even a deer will. As long as you repeat this procedure every time you hunt in a certain spot, you will maintain normal animal activity around you. It tends to keep the deer off balance.''

Many bowhunters can attest to puzzling experiences that have occurred while they watched a buck heading for their stand or shooting lane. For many, wind was right and they hadn't moved a muscle, but for some unknown reason, the animal suddenly stopped, only to reverse directions and walk away, seemingly unalarmed. Some individuals think this is a sixth sense that only super bucks have developed. According to Keller, this sixth-sense theory is hogwash. He says it isn't what a buck scents that causes him to retreat—it's what he doesn't scent.

"If you pollute an area with your scent, or you overuse an area," Keller says, "other animals in the vicinity will avoid it. Then, what you've got is a pocket, or vacuum, with no natural animal scent to it. Bucks seem to pick up on this without any problem.''

This method of scouting and hunting the does' bedroom is deadly during the pre-rut and post-rut period, when most does are not in estrus. During the peak of the rutting cycle, though, it is not a good place to hunt. Then, the bucks will be making and visiting scrapes, and the "hot" does will be seeking them out, or at least availing themselves to the bucks where the bucks have set up shop. This calls for a change in tactics. Now you want to set up in the more traditional, commonly accepted places to hunt deer in the fall: over trails leading to and from scrapes.

The peak rut period lasts for about 10 days to two weeks. If you haven't scored by then, you still have an excellent opportunity awaiting you at the does' bedroom. Hunt it like you did during the pre-rut period, and chances are good that you'll have some decent bucks to choose from. A few more does will go into estrus later on in December, and the bucks will be primed for their last chance at servicing a receptive doe.

It takes a couple of seasons for this routine to sink in, but when it finally does, things are never the same on the back 40.

6

Beaver Pond Bucks

But what if there is no farm country in your area or you can't get permission to hunt it. Many hunters pursue the big ones in more wooded areas and in specific places within those areas.

Successful big buck hunter Dick Pearson believes in hunting deep woods bucks, but he fine-tunes that. He credits his consistent success to a good beaver pond. I couldn't agree with him more.

My own exploits, and those of every member of my hunting party, more than support Pearson's contention. Of 30 bucks taken within the last eight years at my hunting camp, at least half have involved some sort of beaver pond skullduggery. During this time period, I have watched average hunters become capable deer slayers, and have heard many first-buck stories that include beaver ponds—my kid brother's 200-pound, eight-pointer last year; my brother-in-law's first buck after a 10-year drought hunting elsewhere; my nephew's and two neighbors' first bucks.

Surprisingly, this hotspot of hotspots is not only common in every geographic area of the nation, but it is overlooked and untapped by most sportsmen. Only trappers, a few smart duck hunters and a handful of energetic trout fishermen have tested beaver ponds. But deer hunters, I dare say, have the most to gain. One beaver pond buck taken in Alabama is the largest typical to have come from the Southeast to date, scoring 187⅝ Boone & Crockett points.

"First off, a beaver pond is the only natural barrier that truly bottlenecks a whitetail deer," Pearson explains. "Nothing so drastically affects their movement patterns. And I mean nothing.

"Second, a beaver pond is the only reprieve a deer can get from insects which literally drive deer buggy in many areas of the country. This can be a legitimate part of any bowhunter's early season strategy if he knows how to exploit it.

"Third, ponds are reliable sources of water, which bucks need during the rut—more so than most hunters care to believe. Again, this is another factor affecting practical hunting strategy, only it comes into play later in the hunting season.

"Fourth, they're some of the best areas to consider for the use of artificial scent trails because the hunter can control his own scent by traveling in or along the edge of the water. The reason most hunters don't do so well with sex scents is the contamination factor—in the process of attempting to use a commercial scent, they almost invariably leave behind their own scent. Beaver ponds can be a godsend.

"And fifth, a good beaver pond is like a Christmas present to a deer because the thick cover surrounding the pond comes in the same wrapper as food and safety. What more could a whitetail want?"

In spite of the many first-buck and monster-buck stories floating around, hunting beaver ponds requires just as much deer lore and woodsmanship as any other hunting method. But you will definitely get out of it what you put into it. The weekend hunter is bound to see more four-legged visitors near his stand if he hunts near a beaver pond, and a serious hunter, Pearson feels, could have his best shot at a trophy buck here.

At our camp, some common sense and, perhaps, a little uncommon persistence has led to success rates that keep getting better each year. And new twists to old methods add more enjoyment to the hunt. I recall the very first time we set foot on our new piece of deer real estate. We found a huge pond that didn't appear on any topographic map or aerial photo. Elated, we put two portables up—one at the dam and one at the outlet. One of the spots was an instant hit, and it remained hot for years. The other never did pan out. We eventually discovered that the nonproductive end was too open, and a better stand area was farther down the creek.

Then there's that main trail that circles the pond; it's the kind of trail you will find around every beaver pond. Often, these

"A good beaver pond is like a Christmas present to a deer," said Dick Pearson, "because the thick cover surrounding the pond comes in the same wrapper as food and safety."

well-traveled runways are as deep as six inches, appearing to be etched in braille. If you are interested in does and yearling bucks, go ahead and hunt these trails. Mature bucks? Except for a very short period during a segment of the rut, consider these trails a waste of time.

So, there are rules to the game. But first, how do you find beaver ponds in good deer country? And are some ponds better than others?

The starting point is a large, general map showing the drainage pattern of the area you intend to hunt. Sources are numerous. National and state forest maps are good springboards. The hydrology maps that most state natural resources agencies keep on file are good, too. Also, the agricultural extension and soil conservation district offices keep updated maps of the overall drainage system, and these maps display soil types as well.

These soil maps can be especially helpful. They are the secret tools of several trophy hunters I know. These hunters use the maps to identify pockets that might hold large-rack bucks. How? Listings of where record-book bucks have been taken often reveal patterns involving certain counties. And research has shown that, although genetics is important, nutrition has more impact on antler development. Soils are the key. Those with some calcium and phosphorus that are not overly acidic should be looked at first. Ask the soil scientist to identify the better soils in the region.

While examining these general maps look for trends. Which way does the water flow? Where are all the better soils? Are there any roadless areas? Where might the high grounds be in relation to swamps? How is the ownership distributed?

The next step is the topographic or U.S. Geological Survey quadrangle map. To get the most out of these maps, you will need to know your beaver basics. As an example, you can eliminate those portions on the map where the contour lines are very close together, indicating rapid changes in elevation. Any stream that bisects these areas will not be dammed because the terrain is too steep to hold ponds. And the flat bogs, which are indicated by the marsh symbols, can also be rejected, as the vegetative cover is most likely to be alder, black spruce or cedar; beavers feed almost exclusively on aspen and birch when given a choice.

Small streams, where most beaver ponds are constructed, show up on the map as single blue lines. But where a pond has been built, the stream will "read" as a double line that is colored-in solid blue. And if the contour map has been updated within the past several years, photo corrections will show up in purple, with the double lines indicating a recent beaver pond. That's all there is to it.

Aerial photographs taken under sunny skies also show ponds well. The light reflects off the water's surface, and in the photograph, this will catch the eye of even the untrained map reader.

Unfortunately, aerial surveys are not taken with the regularity that many big buck hunters like to see, so don't rule out an area if the last photographic flight was taken more than eight to 10 years ago. Various forestry agencies—federal, state and county—are good sources for these maps because they rely on the maps to keep up with timber inventories.

Besides maps, people can lead you to these deer hotspots. Biologists for public utilities companies, which must comply with mandated federal and state regulations, inventory beaver populations while preparing environmental impact statements. And loggers are always helpful. But your best bet is going to the local game warden. In many states, wardens are charged with the responsibility of controlling the activities of beavers, ensuring that beaver handiwork won't endanger safe passage of the motoring public. In my area, the local warden seems to get wind of a new beaver pond before it begins to fill up because he's got the county highway department on his case every spring. Ask the conservation officer in your area, and hope that he's uninitiated to the game of beaver pond bucks.

Beaver ponds, like people, come in assorted shapes and sizes. Some are long and slender, some are short and squat, some are old and some are young. You have to know how to handle each one if your strategy is going to work.

For example, determining the age of a pond can be important. Generally, the newer the pond, the better. Both resident deer and those traveling through the area tend to skirt the pond, and they cross, without much hesitation, near the dam and the outlet at the other end of the pond. Find a brand-new impoundment, and you might have an instant hotspot—occasionally, at both ends. But if the area gets thinned out by bucktoothed buzz saws, the deer gradually steer wider and wider from the ends.

Both abandoned and active ponds, however, are worthy of further investigation; ponds far outlive their makers, and edges could still be deer magnets if the pond is relatively deep and choked with cover. I've even seen bucks move in on older pond sites once the second-growth vegetation had taken over.

In areas like this the bucks lie with their backs to the water, watching their backtrails. And in routine fashion, they will ignore wind direction because they know they can't get "blind-sided" by any predator approaching from the water.

Even former ponds affect hunter strategy and success. One fall, well downstream from an active pond Pearson had been monitoring, he found the remains of an old pond that had long since been drained. That season, he avoided hunting around it, reasoning that the large opening in the forest wouldn't necessarily force deer around the drained area or keep them from racing across it if they really had to. But the following year, he made a discovery that really opened his eyes. It taught him yet another unusual twist that makes deer hunting an ever-learning, ever-challenging sport.

While backtracking a large set of tracks from an active beaver pond, Pearson was led straight to the old pond basin. He hadn't actually walked over it that season, as he had merely glanced at it from afar. "I was amazed," he told me. "The ground was really stampeded with tracks. At first, I thought the deer might have been breeding there at night.

"Slowly, I began to unravel the mystery. I walked the entire basin, and I found a few tender green plants shooting up from the silty bottomland. This must have been the last green meal left in the woods because killing frosts had set in several weeks earlier. It then became a simple matter of figuring out where to intercept the deer as they approached the area. I ended up letting a decent eight-pointer and a smaller 10-pointer go by before I saw the buck I'm still chasing. Next year, though..."

So the deer were grazing at their salad bar, but just how significant is this to a hunter? Was it a fluke, or do deer ordinarily respond to this phenomenon?

"It's commonplace," Pearson said. "I'll prove it." Then he lead me out to his yard on the side of his house, which is hidden deep in the Chippewa National Forest of north-central Minnesota. On that cold December day, there were several inches of snow on the lawn, but I could see patches where the tips of green blades poked through the white crusted surface. I could also see plenty of deer tracks.

"I just had my septic tank pumped out last week," he explained. "In a matter of days, I'd bet more than two dozen deer were feeding here at night, right next to the house. As you can see, green grass sprouted wherever some effluent had been spilled, and

Both abandoned and active ponds are worthy of further investigation. Ponds far outlive their makers, and the edges can still be deer magnets if the pond is relatively deep and choked with cover.

it sure didn't take long for the deer to find out about it!''

A beaver pond's orientation has a definite bearing on how concentrated travel lanes are apt to be. In the northern latitudes, for instance, ponds that run east and west are preferred by hunters, as opposed to those running north and south. Due to the prevailing winds in these latitudes, general travel patterns of deer will be in a northerly or southerly direction. When they hit the east-and-west pond, deer are much more likely to bend around it near the dam or the outlet so they can continue on their northerly or southerly path, rather than continue in an easterly or westerly direction once they are forced either way by the water. This doubles a hunter's odds of seeing deer at these intersections.

But the east-and-west beaver pond can be improved. The granddaddy of all bottlenecks is where you find a pond running east and west with another natural barrier—a large river, a lake, a major highway, even a swamp—close by, to one side or the other. Now, you've got a bottleneck on a large scale and one on a small scale; deer might be channeled from the larger barrier to the closest side of the pond (where you'll be waiting). This is one of the refinements we've discovered at out deer camp, where the beavers are logging a small tributary of a large river. The area between the river and the pond has produced more deer than any other, even though it always has much less deer sign.

Another thing to keep on the lookout for is a colony of beavers that has constructed a series of dams. Once the animals have exhausted their food supply, they'll move up or down the creek bed if the tree cover is suitable, constructing more dams in the process. Sometimes, they'll be fairly close to the original pond, giving the enterprising hunter added options for stands that take advantage of double and even triple bottlenecks.

I bowhunt an area in northern Wisconsin that is an exact replica of this setup. There is a large meadow where the first beaver pond was built in the area about 25 years ago. To the east, there is a new pond that was built just last summer. To the west, there is one that was built a few years ago. I have ace-in-the-hole stands situated between each pond.

But it isn't always that simple. I have watched similar dam networks being built and have dreamed about the increased odds of deer travel in the area, only to be disappointed. I've spent many autumn days overlooking an area that, at first glance, should have been ideal, but that was actually void of deer—including does and yearlings. Apparently, if the travel lanes are too constricted or the

This bowhunter will have the best chance of bagging a big buck if he stays in his ground blind, which is situated next to a natural bottleneck caused by the open field behind the hunter and the river (not pictured) in front of the hunter. The granddaddy of all bottlenecks is the spot where you find a pond running east and west with another natural barrier to one side.

landscape is too tangled with felled trees, the deer tend to avoid the area. Like any other aspect of deer hunting, you have to pay your dues.

One of the bonuses of hunting around beaver ponds, as Dick Pearson mentioned earlier, is the hunter's ability to control and render human scent harmless. By donning a pair of hipboots or waders, a hunter on his way to a stand can often chart an entry trail that literally leaves no scent behind for the deer to detect. Think about this. How many doors does this open? I can think of at least four.

First, you can sprinkle doe mating scent from the water onto trails near the water's edge without giving yourself away. Then, you can double back or circle around to a strategically located stand situated on the other side of the trail.

Second, you can use a Belly Boat or canoe to cross the pond and get to a stand overlooking one of the bottlenecks without leaving a scent trail behind in the area you expect the deer to be coming from. And you can do it quietly. Thus, a gun hunter could cover both the dam and the outlet of a small pond from a centrally located stand with confidence, knowing that either side could produce.

Third, if you're an early season hunter in bug country, you can set up from a flooded tree and wait it out for deer bathing at dusk.

And fourth, you can simply use the wind to disperse your scent across the pond. Portable stands can be moved around as wind directions dictate. For instance, when hunting an east-and-west pond with a northerly wind, hunt the north side. Or hunt the west side of a north-and-south pond during westerly winds.

Incidentally, the one time to hunt over that main beaten path is when bucks are in their head-shaking, full-rut state. Then, when a hot doe zips along the trail, even a mature buck will use the path. I've seen bucks with tails erect and noses to the ground, trotting stiff-legged right over a doe's scent trail. They look like trolley cars on a roller coaster, jerking this way and that as the tracks ahead dictate. At any other time of the year, though, it pays to back off and look for faint trails.

What happens if the pond freezes over? It loses some of its magic, but the deer will still be hesitant to cross the pond during daylight hours. But, by freeze-up, you should have already scored on your buck. After all, you've got the animals cornered, and there are a lot of things going your way—especially the deer.

Provided you find a tree that hasn't been gnawed down, your portable treestand can give you the best vantage point to watch over a beaver pond. That's how the author took this big buck.

Beaver Pond Points To Ponder

Beaver, which are the largest rodents in North America, can alter the landscape and affect deer movement patterns for many years following. But knowing a few beaver basics can keep you ahead of the game.

1)Beaver build ponds ranging from 100 to 2,000 feet in length, averaging eight to 20 feet in depth.

2)They eat 22 to 30 ounces of tree bark per day, and fell 200 to 300 trees (many of which do not fall toward the pond) in a single year.

3) They anchor trees and branches to the bottoms of the ponds for winter food supplies, thus making travel across the pond difficult even for the swift white-tailed deer.

4)They construct dams that far outlast the useful life of the pond.

5)Colonies of beavers usually move on in three to five years.

6)When abandoned dams break, the ponds drain and often become lush green meadows.

7)Beaver sometimes construct a series of dams and create networks of ponds, especially if the terrains surrounding the creek beds are heavily wooded and the slopes are not too steep.

8)They are nocturnal creatures, working from dusk to dawn; hunters who don't see any near a particular pond shouldn't automatically assume that the pond is abandoned.

9)Beaver have few natural enemies. In the early 1950s, when beaver numbers were extremely high, an outbreak of tularemia hit. Today, beaver populations across most of the nation are considered quite high and they continue to escalate.

Deep Woods Deer

One of the most pleasurable pursuits on the face of the earth is the challenge of hunting white-tailed deer in a wilderness setting. No other scene so captivates a hunter. The romantic image of a stately buck in a deep, wooded forest seems to be the quintessence of the sport. For some, it is the only place to hunt deer.

Now the deep woods may be serene. It may be enchanting. It might even seem electric as you melt into a "oneness with nature." But in spite of all its charm, it remains one of the most difficult places to hunt whitetails, yet one of the best big buck producing areas in all of deer hunting. And those caught up with idealistic fantasies about this "deer heaven" are most likely to become victims of the forest—delusioned, frustrated, defeated. Why? Because there are more obstacles than opportunities awaiting the serious deer hunter in the deep woods.

Take the fall breeding season, as an example. In farm country, or areas with woodlots broken up by fields and croplands, deer populations are much higher and more concentrated. That means you not only know where most of the deer are likely to be spending a good portion of their time, but you know where the bucks are going to be looking for does in estrus. Conversely, research has shown that in forested areas—where deer numbers are lower and less concentrated—deer movements, especially bucks chasing does during the rut, are more numerous and erratic. Thus, the deer are more difficult to pattern; yesterday's hotspot could become today's dead spot.

Over the years, I have boiled my personal strategy down to observing two simple rules for the game of hunting deer in the unbroken forest. They aren't shortcuts. And they're far from being a quick-fix. But if you study them and apply them conscientiously to the right conditions near you, your odds will be greatly improved.

Rule 1: Hunt Where Deer, Not Hunters, Go

This first rule is so ridiculously simple, many hunters overlook it. It really hit me one day when a deep woods deer slayer, Arvo Hoppala, finally revealed to me his secret for killing big bucks year after year, no matter what conditions prevailed.

"It's like this," he said, as he whittled on a walking stick from a diamond willow. "All I do is look for places where the deer are and the hunters ain't."

Although I knew he was onto something legitimate, it took another year to translate Hoppala's Finlander wisdom into deer hunter English. One day late in the season, I followed his tracks in the snow to see just where he had spent the day. They led me into the thickest tag alder swamp I'd ever crawled through. So he hunts snarled swamps, I thought. Is that all there is to it? But the tracks never stopped. I knew Hoppala didn't sneak hunt, so I continued following his trail and made the deer discovery of a lifetime.

Gradually the land began to rise, and the alders gave way to popples and a few scattered balsams. Here, in the middle of nowhere, there was a two-acre knoll, an island of high ground buttressed by a swamp. And was this little piece of real estate ever laced with fresh deer sign! Before long, I came upon a blood trail. I had found the exact spot where that rascal Hoppala had set up his stand and had shot a deer. As I surveyed the situation, all the pieces of the puzzle began to fall into place: the deer that entered this island were like kings in a moated castle. They had a sure-fire reprieve from two-legged predators, and any four-legged enemy approaching them from the swamp could easily be detected, no matter which way the wind blew. What really irritated me was that I had known about swamp islands from previous hunts in other states; somehow, I had forgotten about the universality of this hotspot.

If you plan to be a successful deep woods hunter, you'll probably need help bringing your deer all the way back to the road. If you hunt solo, let a responsible friend know where you'll be.

Arvo Hoopala's secret for killing big bucks: "All I do is look for places where the deer are and the hunters ain't."

For three years the author's friend took nice bucks with his bow from the same tree stand. Then one year he got skunked; the wind had changed direction.

Swamp islands have become my best deer-getter in big woods. When I scout for new deer hotspots, they are constantly in the forefront of my mind. How do I locate them? Scouring the countryside surely won't hurt, but maps can save a lot of time and put you into the lap of several such deer sanctuaries with much less effort.

The time-honored topographic map can be extremely helpful if you know how to "read" swamp islands. And not just any old swamp island is going to be a deer magnet during the deer season. Here's what to look for:

First, pick out the swamps that aren't too vast and aren't far from good deer habitat. A two- to three-square-mile lowland area, bounded on at least two sides by recently cut high ground is ideal. Bigger swamps adjacent to mature forests, where there is little understory growth and few clear-cuts, won't be nearly as productive.

Second, look for islands within the swamp. These isolated patches of higher ground will show up where a contour line suddenly appears as a small circle, or perhaps a double-ringed doughnut-like object. Remember, the rest of the swamp is low and flat and there will be no contour lines unless there is a change in elevation. But if there is any relief to the surface features, the contour lines will tattle on it.

Aerial photos also squeal on these deer hotspots. But unlike topographic maps, they may be difficult to locate for some areas. The best sources for both maps would be a governmental unit with some jurisdiction over the region. That may be a national forest, the Bureau of Land Management, the Soil Conservation Service, a state forest or a county administering tax-forfeited lands. Natural resource agencies with a forestry division are usually the first place I head for—a trip in person to the appropriate office headquarters or field office could save time, money and frustration in the long run. Be sure to have the legal description of the prospective areas you intend to look into before you pound on any doors.

Hunting swamp islands can be tricky. Some are unapproachable when the winds blow from certain quadrants due to your access route and that of the deer. My neighbor is a case in point. For three straight years, he shot a buck with his bow from the same stand by hunting hard on weekends. Then one year he got zipped. He finally realized that in a "normal" year his swamp island could be virtually infallible, but when contrary winds blew it was impossible for him to gain access to his island without alerting the deer to his presence. If only he had a few backup islands for those days.

The second place hunter pressure can be all but avoided is along navigable rivers. Two hunters with two cars can pull a most effective maneuver by dropping one car off at the take-out point, and doubling back to the put-in. Canoes, prams and car-toppers are the perfect tool to get you into the interior sectors of areas where deer are seldom confronted by humans. But these deer aren't stupid. They're just easier to outsmart than those who have learned survival tactics and use their senses overtime.

Hunting strategy on rivers is a matter of personal choice, blended with the conditions at hand. If there are numerous oxbows and the river meanders like a bear with a belly-full of fermented blueberries, I'd be inclined to recline in one of the seats and see

Richard Builta and his son Greg have taken these and other whitetails through teamwork and patterning food alleys.

what I could happen onto. Rivers with numerous rapids, on the other hand, should be utilized primarily to get into the the hinterland. I have two bowhunter friends who are very successful river-bank hunters. All they do is stillhunt the main deer trails that run along the water's edge. The gurgling water deadens any sound they make, and the deer often come to the edge of the stream to drink during the day. The point is, you want to go with the flow and adapt to whatever you have to work with. Just don't bite off more than you can chew or you could end up coming off the water under the wrap of total darkness, which can be avoided with a little pre-hunt planning.

Rule 2: Pattern Food Alleys

Normally, hunting specific feeding areas is a waste of time in the deep woods. One research study, involving the stomach analysis of hundreds of deer, revealed that deer eat an amazingly wide variety of plants—about 70, in total. And the food source occurring the most, aspen leaves, is so common in the woods that

When you've dragged as many deer from the deep woods as Noble Carlson has, you learn the value of friends, especially those with dozers and skidders that make deer hauling easy.

it provides the discriminating hunter with next to nothing to go on. But this doesn't mean deer prefer 70 different kinds of food sources. When given a choice, as we discussed in Chapter 2, there is one that always tops the list: acorns.

Your best bet is to find small pockets of oaks in league with a water source, dense cover for good bedding areas and a swamp or two for heavy-duty deer survival tactics against hunter intrusions.

When you find such a place, you'll have deer in the immediate area during the day. Then, it becomes a simple matter to scrutinize the shape of the oak stand, looking for fingers that lead into heavy cover.

That's pretty close to where the first deer coming to feed at dusk, or leaving at dawn, are going to appear. You must get to your stand way ahead of time, however, and plan on waiting it out well beyond the time you expect the deer to be on the move if you intend to continue hunting that spot.

Your best bet to finding deep woods deer is to locate small pockets of oaks that are close to water and heavy cover. That's where this Alabama hunter found this nice buck.

Slashings from logging operations offer another reliable deer magnet in the deep woods. Slashings are to forest deer what crop fields are to deer in farm country. They're the most nutritional source of food available, and the deer know it. In order for whitetails to survive a harsh winter in the northern tiers of their range, they must put on heavy reserves of fat, and herbacious plants provide more protein and calories than woody browse. Forest openings are more vital than browse, providing lush green vegetation when the deer need it most, just before killing frost and in late spring.

So if you can find a secluded slashing that has remained undisturbed by hunters, you're going to be on top of a major food source that can also be hunted intelligently. The best way to pull it off is to borrow a page from corn country deer hunters and glass these slashings from a distance, rather than going right in and risk being detected by the deer. From several evenings spent studying exactly where deer come out into the open areas to feed, you can put together a strategy for stand locations—and entry routes—so the deer walk into an ambush without being tipped off. They should continue in their feeding patterns—usually at dusk—as long as green plant material is available.

Incidentally, studies conducted by noted ruffed grouse authority, Gordon Gullion, show that aspen leaves on popple suckers withstand harsh frosts longer than any other forest vegetation. Deer will key in on them where available, which translates into more deer hunting savvy. Seek out not only new slashings from the previous summer, but one- and two-year-old logging disturbances where aspen shoots are likely to have flowered at the heights deer can reach.

Locating slashings is easy. Just ask around. Pulp operators are listed in the local yellow pages of your telephone directory, as are companies associated with the timber products industry. Also, look up small-time loggers in the classified "want ads" section of local newspapers. Their ads will be listed under "firewood for sale." Most of these sources will tell you exactly where they've been cutting, and you can chart their whereabouts on a map. Perhaps you can cook up a routine that allows you to monitor them efficiently without spending a lot of time behind the wheel of your car.

Deep woods deer hunting is rewarding even when you come home empty-handed. For many, filling a deer tag once every four or five years is icing on the cake. Doing it year after year? That would be a dream come true. But once you learn to recognize these factors that draw deer to certain areas, you won't have to dream about it any more. You can do it.

8

Aggressive Stand Hunting

Once you've decided on the geographical location in which to
pursue a trophy, there are a number of options as to the
technique you will use to collect that big buck. After all, there's
more to harvesting a real wall-hanger than just plopping yourself
down in a likely looking spot.

One of the most popular methods used by today's whitetail
hunters involves the use of a tree stand. And I'll be the first to
admit that I didn't always know as much about this type of hunting
as I do now. As a matter of fact, Elmer Fudd reminds me of the
kind of deer hunter I used to be. I couldn't even fool a silly rabbit
consistently, much less a wary whitetail. But that was 20 years
ago. Since then, I've learned that people who bag a buck every
year aren't just lucky; they're doing something the "less
fortunate" are not. Arvo Hoppala, that deer slayer mentioned in
Chapter 7, hunts by a rule that separates the luckless from the
skilled.

"If you hunt like everybody else," he said, "you won't see the
deer they don't."

Beg your pardon?

Well, there's gold beneath Hoppala's Finlander double-talk,
but you have to dig for it. Take stand hunting. For many, it's a
simple, runway-watching affair. Find a well-used trail, set up shop
downwind and wait it out for the big buck to show. Right?

Unfortunately, it doesn't quite work out that way. There are too many variables involved that can screw things up.

Stand hunting is, without a doubt, the most effective way to bag a buck for most people. But why are some hunters more effective than others? What is the real secret to success? The secret is that stand hunters shouldn't just passively stand around. Instead, they should use a system carefully designed to eliminate weak links. By critically evaluating every facet of your system, you'll soon see where the weak links are and learn how to turn them into strengths. That's the essence of aggressive stand hunting.

Sounds simple, but let's go beyond the Elmer Fudd stage. Let's dig deeper and look at the three components of stand hunting that demand close scrutiny: the area, the stand itself and the tactics. None of these facets of stand hunting can be overlooked if you expect to fill that deer tag every year, especially if you're after a trophy buck.

The Area

Actually, where to hunt is easier to master than how to hunt. I look at stand placement as a function of only two factors: identifying places deer must—not may—cross, and identifying those areas deer tend to cross more often than others. A good example of the first would be a physical constraint that serves to funnel deer through a narrow path of travel. As I've mentioned, rivers, lakes, beaver ponds, swamps, fields, bluffs and highways are obvious obstacles, and deer tend to avoid them or skirt their edges.

More subtle, but just as productive, are areas in which a hunter can double the odds. Instead of overlooking one deer trail, for instance, pick a place where two intersect. Instead of monitoring a scrape, try to find a fresh one near a bedding or feeding area. A discerning eye can pick these up, but the casual observer will not. It's a matter of digging a little.

This reminds me of a stand area at my deer camp that has paid off virtually every year. The only problem was that the deer I sighted, besides does, were invariably young bucks. Four spikes and a forkhorn were taken there in four consecutive years. There were always large rubs and scrapes in the vicinity, but where were the big bucks?

My restlessness and a burning desire to learn more helped me find out. Over the next three years, I took a ten-, a nine- and an eight-pointer within a few hundred yards of the old hotspot.

The author believes a buck uses less traveled trails more than most other deer throughout most of the year. But when the rut is on, bucks will be on main trails more often as they pursue does.

What I learned—by a tedious trial-and-error process—is that big bucks don't use the same areas as do lesser bucks and does. Big-buck trails are rarely well-worn, as the real bruisers take different routes each time through an area, rather than use a specific runway. So, when I scout an area where I can double up, I look for individual buck tracks going in the same general direction, instead of heavily used trails. The only time a buck may use these more obvious runways is if the absolute peak of the rut is on and he's tracking a doe in estrus. But that's a mighty big "if."

By day, bucks hang out near, but not in, heavy cover unless they are pressed by danger. By night, they will roam open ridges and riverbank edges in search of does. Don't let large prints in the latter areas fool you. Instead, try to find an area that's secure and somewhat secluded. The northwestern corner of a swamp, where north/south and east/west travel is likely to occur, is a classic example.

Today's hunters can benefit from modern technology for fine-tuning their stand placement by using trail watchers. In the old days, we used to string sewing thread across a deer trail to see whether it was being used regularly. It had to be checked often, however, or the time of day when the string was broken by a passing deer could not be determined. That meant continually returning to the area and thus spreading our scent around, which could virtually shut down a big-buck hotspot. Instead, I now use a trail watching timed device that has a 24-hour clock. As long as I'm careful not to use it more than one time on a given trail, and avoid spreading scent from my hands to the instrument (surgical gloves help), I get good results.

The Stand

To set up your portable stand location without being detected by a smart buck, you'll have to overcome the three S's: sight, sound and smell.

Deer are visually alerted to your presence by movement or simple suspicion. For this reason, a stand should, if at all possible, be situated in front of some sort of backdrop. Last year, I gained a renewed appreciation of this important principle, and the lesson cost me a shot at a good buck.

I was in a portable tree stand, about 20 feet up in a big aspen. The year before, I had taken a big-bodied nine-pointer from that same tree, so I was quite confident that deer couldn't see me that far up. I was wrong.

Not more than 15 minutes after sunrise, on the firearms opener, a doe suddenly materialized below me. Almost immediately, she looked up, right at me. And from the moment our eyes met, she was as jumpy as a jitterbug, even though the wind was coming from her direction. After the traditional bobbing-of-the-head and foot-stomping routine, she bolted. A good buck was with her, and I didn't see him until he bounded away on her trail. I could have avoided this mistake by simply moving my portable 20 yards to one side, to take advantage of a nearby balsam to break up my outline.

What if you don't have a large tree nearby to disguise your silhouette? One trick is to hunt from behind the tree. That way, the deer won't see you until he's right on top of you. I've done this with both permanent and portable tree stands.

Although you want to keep movement to a minimum, it's difficult to keep your hands perfectly still for hours on end. Do the next best thing—refrain from wearing a pair of Blaze Orange hunting gloves, the kind that go on sale each fall. It's best to wear camo gloves instead. They'll hide minor movements rather than telegraph them.

The direction in which the stand faces, from the shooter's point of view, is also important. Bowhunters should never hunt straight ahead because they won't be able to make a full draw without bending sideways at the waist. This alone has caused many arrows to fall short of their intended target. Gun hunters should also avoid facing the area where the deer are expected to travel, because it is far easier for a right-hander to survey the area to his left and get off a quick shot than to swing over his right shoulder.

One of the most common mistakes stand hunters make is to rely on a single stand to hunt a particular spot. You can't count on prevailing winds to come out of the west or the northwest every day.

Quite often, in fact, a period of Indian summer-like weather prevails in the fall. Then, weak high pressure systems linger with southerly breezes. Winds from the other quadrants don't last as long, so you won't need four stands to hunt an area effectively, just two: one for northwest winds and one for those southerlies.

The exact height of the stand should be determined by how far up you need to go to get above the understory. States vary considerably on laws restricting tree stand heights, so be sure to check regulations in the state you are hunting. Typically, portables are not as restricted as permanent stands.

The final decision of which tree(s) you use should depend upon whether you are bowhunting or rifle hunting and whether you are using a permanent stand or a portable one. Gun hunters can "lay back" a bit, but they should prune sight lines to increase the coverage area. Besides accuracy, the major advantage of the modern rifle is range. Where legal, bowhunters should prune tree branches that can impede draw or arrow flight. Only once did I make the mistake of trying to bowhunt out of a stand originally built for gun hunting. I can still see the buck looking back at me after my elbow bumped into one of the tree's branches.

Building a permanent stand? A few tricks can go a long way. First, don't spend any more time than necessary on-site building your stand. I take a pocket-sized notebook with me and record all of the measurements I'll need for the braces, the floor, the seat and a railing which is a good idea for safety as well as a gun rest. Then, I get the heck out of there. All of the parts are cut and fitted away from the site, then brought in later and assembled as quickly and quietly as humanly possible. It usually takes only 20 minutes.

Also, be sure to camouflage the sized lumber with spray paint well ahead of the season so that the paint's odors have had a chance to dissipate. A piece of rigid foam is a good idea for the floor and seat, to cut down on heat loss. A small section of burlap placed over the foam (the burlap should be carried into the woods and out with you each day) is the final touch to a comfortable and quiet elevated hideout. Although popular, I don't use carpeting because it introduces foreign odors and will get crunchy underfoot if a freeze follows a rain. My brother-in-law takes it a step further and even adds a roof. We call his favorite stand "The High-Rise."

The purchase of a portable tree stand can be a baffling experience; there are so many kinds and styles from which to choose. There isn't a particular model that's perfect for everyone because individual needs vary considerably. But there are some helpful guidelines.

The best stand for the average hunter is the lightweight portable kind that utilizes tree climbers or screw-in type steps. If you're concerned about tree damage, purchase steps that are attached to trees via straps. I've tried dozens of stands, the non-climbing, lock-on stands get high marks in my book. Be sure that your stand comes with a safety belt. It is an absolute necessity for any tree stand.

Hunters with a low center of gravity, however, will have a hard time with the ultra portable models. It takes some dexterity to get in and out of them. For the heavy-set deer hunter, climbing tree stands are good. They can be noisy to set up, but climbing with them is easier.

Texas-style ladder stands are handy for areas near prairies and roadways. However, getting a ladder through the deep woods is another matter.

The Tactics

Besides stand location and selection, your entry methods must also come under the magnifying glass. No stone should be left unturned when it comes to minimizing, or eliminating, the spread of human scent upon your entry.

Most seasoned hunters know that rubber boots are superior to leather ones for this, and I consider this a requirement, not an option.

Bucks only get this big by being smart, and that means they know how to use the wind! To get a shot at a buck like this one, you'll need two stands. One for northwest winds and one for those southerlies.

But rubber boots can be cold and are slippery when wet, so I carry a pair of warmer, insulated packs over my shoulder and change into them when I set up shop. These "deer hunting-only" boots will have been cured in a scent-controlled environment, along with all of my deer hunting clothes.

Some equally vital considerations are often overlooked. Gore-Tex gloves, for example, are breathable as well as well as waterproof—a solid choice for any hunter. Unfortunately, as the moisture escapes, so does scent from your hands. Fishermen have been made aware of the fish-repelling amino acid L-Serine, which is present in human fingerprints, but hunters should also be aware of butyric acid, also found in human fingerprints, which reportedly repels mammals.

The solution for scent-proofing your hands is similar to the one for your feet—keep them clean and wear rubber gloves on the way in and as you ascend your stand. For the rest of your clothing, the best precautions are frequent washings in baking soda with plenty of air-drying time, and getting out of them the moment you leave the woods. I store mine in large plastic trash buckets, the kind with airtight lids.

Scents? Although I subscribe to the best-scent-is-no-scent philosophy, I won't categorically rule out deer lures. You've read enough on the subject. But masking scents are another matter. It takes some logical forethought to get anything of real hunting value out of them.

For example, you shouldn't wear any critter scent and hunt from a tree unless the scent bearer also climbs trees. Common sense tells me that, but I can't count the number of tree stand hunters I've seen with fox, skunk and even buck scent on their clothes. About the only true "masking animal scent" that could be worn in a tree is coon scent, but it can't really overcome or disguise odor from human bacteria. In fact, coon scent may even draw attention to you from below.

Natural, non-food earthen scents, such as pine or cedar, are better for clothes. But while on the ground, coon scent or fox urine conservatively applied to your boots makes sense—if you can remove it and leave it at the base of a nearby tree. The scent of an intelligent but innocuous predator in the area may give the deer a false sense of security.

The major advantage of elevated stands, apart from offering a better vantage point, is getting your scent up and away from deer below. That advantage is neutralized if these details are ignored.

Making unnatural or excessive noise as you approach your stand is another factor in the system. Brushing out and sweeping clean a footpath—especially the last 100 yards—is a necessary precaution for those who go to their stand before daylight . So is the elimination of a flashlight beam, at least for that final distance. If you'll leave the light off and give your eyes a 20-minute adjustment period, you'll be astonished at how effective your night vision can be. Otherwise, pick a path that's easy and quiet to follow under the cover of darkness. A conifer bog with a carpet of moss is one example. The bank of a creek or river is another.

The major advantage of an elevated stand, apart from offering a better vantage point, is getting your scent up and away from deer below. This buck is unable to pinpoint the foreign odor it senses.

How you hunt from a stand is the final component of your overall strategy. My best advice is to use your own senses to full advantage. I've learned that the key is not looking and listening intently at the same time, but rather concentrating on one sense over the other.

When it's extremely windy, or when there's a soft blanket of snow on the ground, I use my eyes more than my ears. I must look like an owl during the breeding season, as my head slowly turns from left to right and right to left, over and over again. In the process, I pay strict attention to the area behind me. The last three bucks I shot used a blind-side approach. An insulated hat with a bill, rather than a stocking cap, can help cut down on sunlight glare, thus improving visibility.

When the woods are noisy with crunchy leaves, I switch over to my ears. Subconsciously, I try to hear the animal before I see it. It really works if you don't try to use your eyes and ears at the same time.

Aggressive stand hunting can be the most deadly system for outsmarting good bucks year after year. For me, aggressive stand hunting has made the difference between giving my father-in-law his annual Christmas present of venison sausage—and the 50-50 prospect of an empty deer tag.

9

You Can Stand It

What many stand hunters don't realize is that picking the right spot to place a stand is only the first step for success. Staying in that stand, especially when it's cold, can be just as important. What it comes down to is being prepared for the weather. Unfortunately, I had to learn this the hard way.

It was quite a jolt when I first stepped outside the deer shack that morning; the comfortable Indian summer had turned into a frigid winter almost overnight. Just two days ago, the old outdoor thermometer, bearing a faded Marilyn Monroe figure with her classic ruby lipstick smile, had reached a balmy 64 degrees. This morning, she read only 10 degrees.

Undaunted, I forged on. Had to get to that deer stand...running late...overslept.

Although my mind was still groggy from a lousy night's sleep, my step was light and lively. Adrenaline surged through my veins while I recalled all the bucks taken off that tree stand over the years. The only trick was to stay on it all day without coming down for even a moment, for its location was strategically chosen: hunter pressure from the east, north and south could virtually be counted on to push deer along the brushy creek bed that it overlooked. Sooner or later, a buck with my number on it would try to snake by, and experience had taught me that it could be any time of day.

But this day would not go as planned. Instead of being the

victor, I would become a victim, of sort. Oh, a buck came sneaking by all right, and I even got off a decent shot. At least that's what I thought I did. I can't remember the details, although I've tried a million times. To this day, it still plagues me. Only recently, breakthroughs in medical research have helped to unravel the mystery, so there shouldn't be a repeat performance.

What does medicine have to do with deer hunting? A lot. And if you do much hunting from a stand during cool weather, chances are good that you have been or could be victimized as I was.

Dr. Robert Pozos, a nationally known researcher on hypothermia from the University of Minnesota, has studied the human body's defense system with respect to how it copes with extreme cold. From my conversations with him, I think I learned why I missed that buck.

He started by asking a series of probing questions, to which many a hunter would probably have had to say "yes." Were you in a hurry that morning? Did you work up a sweat? Was there a wind? Did you hunt from an elevated stand? Did the weather suddenly turn cold? Did you drink coffee that morning? Did you experience moderate or severe shivering?

"It's really no mystery," he concluded. "You were obviously suffering from the initial stages of hypothermia."

"Hypothermia?!" I said in disbelief. "I thought only lost arctic travelers or drowning victims suffered from that."

"Well, those are the classic cases most often cited," he said. "But you deer hunters are especially vulnerable because you hunt during 'marginal' weather in the fall. Of course, most guys come down from their stands well before succumbing to hypothermia, but it still affects performance and makes life miserable. Hypothermia is a threat when the weather is less severe and you can be caught off guard."

According to Dr. Pozos, temperatures below 40 degrees coupled with a little wind and a wet body are all it takes. That potentially includes an awful lot of hunters across the nation at one time or another, and not just deep woods hackers like me. Fortunately, Dr. Pozos had some practical advice that could help us to stay warm and, hopefully, keep us on our deer stand until that buck drops by.

First, we need to know a few things about heat loss and heat generation. Body heat loss is accomplished primarily through five processes: radiation, conduction, convection, evaporation and respiration. Body heat, on the other hand, is generated by only two

The best way to protect yourself against hypothermia is to dress in layers and avoid sweating. And it's the best way to keep warm on your stand.

means: radiant heat and metabolic rate. Obviously, the two aren't in perfect balance. The whole key is to evaluate each component in an effort to minimize heat loss while maximizing the opportunities for heat generation. By doing this, we can come up with a systematic approach that really works.

Heat Loss

Radiant heat loss is influenced mostly by shape. Heat always flows from warm objects to colder ones, and uniform, spherical objects lose their heat proportionately faster than those that are irregularly shaped.

Tests have shown that billiard balls cool off four times faster than other objects of a similar size and weight. That's why a bare-headed hunter—especially a bald one—who is in the woods without a warm hat or cap is going to get chilled no matter what he's got on his back, hands or feet. Even if you have a head of hair like a Greek god, you won't be much better off; the brain requires 25 percent of the body's hot blood. So, perhaps more serious consideration ought to go into what goes on your head. Stocking caps are popular but, if there is a strong wind, a ski mask under an insulated hat might be a wiser choice.

The neck is often overlooked, but due to the closeness of large arteries there to exposed air, it is just as important as the head. Parkas are best for extreme conditions and, at the very least, a heavy turtleneck dickey, which can be added or removed easily, should be standard gear.

Heat loss by conduction occurs when something cold touches something warm. When deer hunting you simply can't avoid sitting or standing on something that's colder than you are. The best way to handle conduction is to block the heat flow from your fanny and your feet with a good insulator. The most effective material I've found to date is Styrofoam. I carry a two-inch-thick chunk into the woods to sit on and it really helps. Once "broken in," it will conform to my body shape and be quite comfortable. On occasion, it may be necessary to wrap a wool blanket around the Styrofoam to keep noise at a minimum.

Cold feet have caused the not-so-grand exit of many a dedicated stand hunter, and I think that the problem will always be with us. Although most of the problem is physiological, much is psychological.

As Dr. Pozos said, "Some guys can live with pain and some just can't stand it." I'm one who can't, so you can imagine how many different styles of footwear—from Moon Boots to Army-surplus models—I've tried over the years. I know I don't stand alone in this department, yet I see many hunters who will spend $150 on a nice jacket or parka and walk around in a pair of $19.95 specials. Boots are no place to skimp. Felt-lined packs have provided yeoman service for years, and they should be satisfactory for short walks over dry ground.

If you add a pair of Hot Feet insoles to your boots, which were field-tested and recommended by NAHC members, you'll greatly enhance their insulating values. If you still get cold feet with the packs, consider purchasing a pair of Insulated Boot Covers, which NAHC members have also field-tested and approved.

But for longer treks into the backcountry, where swamps and creeks might be encountered, I like the Thinsulate-filled, rubber-soled Guide Boot available from mail order catalogues like Cabela's. They're lightweight, warm and nearly waterproof. When sizing them be sure to go two full sizes larger than your street shoes so two pairs of wool socks can be worn when necessary; too many hunters make the mistake of pinching their toes and reducing vital circulation. By the way, the Hot Feet insoles work wonders with these boots, too.

The Thinsulate/Gore-Tex sock, pioneered by Cabela's, should further increase warmth and dryness. If you stick with regular wool socks, however, be sure to buy them in two sizes, with the smaller one going on first. And by all means carry extras—your feet have over 250,000 sweat glands capable of excreting a half pint of liquid in one day.

Heat loss by convection, or circulation, became well-known in the outdoor community when weather forecasters first started indexing the so-called windchill factor. That was a darn good idea; it's a factor to reckon with.

Who cares if the temperature is going to be 20 degrees tomorrow when the dang wind is going to make it feel like 15 below zero? (That's precisely what a 25-mph wind will do.) Smart deer hunters do two things to thwart the chill of the wind. First, they dress in several layers instead of wearing one or two thick garments. This will not only trap more air—nature's best insulator—but will also provide you with the flexibility to put on and take off clothing as conditions dictate.

Second, by slipping a raincoat under your overcoat, you can cut wind penetration and stay dry, even if it rains. Rainwear made from breathable materials, such as Gore-Tex, would certainly

In this chapter, the author shows you how to dress and equip yourself for staying warm on your stand. Then it's a matter of practicing your shots like this bowhunter is doing.

make sense. This intermediate layer should also include those insulating materials that trap the most air with the least amount of loft, thus increasing maneuverability. Bowhunters, especially, appreciate this.

Traditionally, down has been the top insulator, but there's a little jingle that backpackers like to sing: "Up with down until it gets wet, for then you can bet you've got a threat...yet when it's dry, you'll have few regrets." If getting wet can be a problem where you hunt, consider Thinsulate, pile, Insulite, Bunting or Polar Fleece. These synthetic materials retain their thermal resistance properties even when wet.

Now if the thermometer really plummets when the winds howl, there's no substitute for a quality snowmobile suit. I own two RefrigiWear one-piece suits—a Minus 50 Suit that is perfect for subzero weather, and a Thinsulate Trebark Coveral (#851) for most bowhunting weather.

When the body does get wet, it falls prey to the worst heat-loss mechanism of all—evaporation. A wet body will lose heat 200 times faster than a dry one and, when you combine that with the windchill factor, you've got double trouble. Sweating, a primary cause of evaporation, is the biggest no-no for the deer hunter, said Dr. Pozos.

"If hunters knew how vicious the sweat cycle was," he told me, "they wouldn't take it so lightly."

What's so "vicious" about a little moisture buildup? According to Dr. Pozos, the process starts out as simple water vapor excreted through the skin but, when it reaches the layer of clothing that's below the dew point, it condenses and wets that layer. Latent heat is liberated and released into the air—unfortunately, well away from the skin. Eventually, your clothing wicks the moisture back to your skin, where latent heat is again drawn from your body in order to evaporate the moisture. This goes on until your clothing dries out.

This cycle commands respect, not just mere understanding. Interestingly, the key to its defeat is the long underwear that you put next to your skin, which experts now believe to be the most important component of the anti-cold system. If moisture can be kept away from the skin, most heat loss initiated by evaporation can be eliminated.

For many years, a good wool union suit, for those who could handle the itching, used to be the only undergarment found in deer camps. And wool still makes some sense—its wicking properties

A hat and turtleneck sweatshirt or dickey will help keep you warm by maintaining your core body temperature. Whether you hunt with a gun or bow, wear gloves to keep your hands warm and flexible for the shot. This bowhunter has cut the fingers off his right-hand glove for a cleaner release.

are well documented. But some of the new synthetics do a better job of transmitting moisture—both vapor and liquid—and feel soft to the skin.

Polypropylene, Vinyon, Thermas, Dryline, Thermolite and Hydrofil are some more recent entries. Indeed, these new miracle fabrics do a marvelous job of keeping the skin dry, but the best thing about them is that they can be blended with other "hydrophobic" insulating materials. Lately, I've tried Kenyon Consumer Product's "Comfort Skins" and their new Wool/Thermax blend, and I've learned a valuable lesson: Not all synthetics are created equal. It pays to stick with reputable brand names, such as Kenyon, Gates and Cabela's. Give the new synthetic long underwear a try. You may never go back to that old wool union suit again.

Finally, respiration, or ordinary breathing, can be an important heat-loss factor in cold weather. When you inhale cold air, it is warmed by thousands of tiny blood vessels and brought to 100 percent humidity before it is exhaled. Even here, Dr. Pozos had a few practical recommendations for conserving heat.

Because the lungs have the approximate surface area of a tennis court, they can deliver the moisture needed to condition intake air. But to do that, they need lots of water. Pozos suggested drinking large quantities of water to assist the lungs in that function. Covering your mouth with a scarf or face mask can also cut down on respiratory heat loss.

Heat Generation

On the plus side of the heat loss/heat gain equation, we have only radiant heat and metabolic heat to play with. Radiant heat can only be garnered by placing your stand in a sunny area. Body metabolism, however, is a much more controllable factor, with diet and exercise as its vehicles.

Most kinds of exercise are obviously out of the question. Every buck in the country is going to avoid a red-jacketed figure doing calisthenics in a tree. But you can do isometric contractions of different muscle groups without raising a flag. Just be sure to keep it up for 20-minute intervals or you won't notice any lasting benefits—wiggling toes included.

Another good idea is to hunt out of two stands in fairly close proximity to one another. That way, you can stalk hunt from one location to the other, warming yourself in the process. With two stands, you should also be able to stay on top of the deer without letting them weasel by you when other hunters are likely to be moving them your way.

Diet selection isn't as cut and dried as I once thought it was. Standard advice for combating the cold has been to load up on "high energy" foods—whatever that means. Carbohydrates, such as candy bars, and beverages such as coffee and cocoa are often mentioned. Again, Dr. Pozos had an interesting perspective to offer.

"I have found no scientific basis for recommending sugars as a cold-weather dietary aid," he said. "There may be some empirical or practical evidence that suggests such a course for some individuals, but I'd be tempted to go with more fats than carbohydrates. And I would strongly discourage both coffee and chocolate."

Fats are also a good source of energy, according to commercial fisherman Stanley Sivertson, who has worked the frigid waters of the Great Lakes for more than 50 years. Sivertson eats plenty of oil-rich herring when he is going to be on the water for long periods of time.

Further evidence from research involving Eskimos, who generally eat a lot of foods that have a high fat content, might give credence to Sivertson's theory. In one study, Caucasians and Alaskan Indians were tested to see how long they could keep their hands in 50-degree water. Some Eskimos fell asleep with their hand in the water, while the longest a non-Indian could take it was about one minute!

Liquids should be carefully chosen, too. Recently, the Mayo Clinic in Minnesota confirmed the findings of California's Mount Sinai Medical Center's research on chicken soup: It's not only good, but *good for you* because it is clinically effective in clearing stuffy nasal passages.

Coffee and chocolate are bad for one simple reason: They have significant amounts of caffeine, which blocks a hormone that enables the body to restrain urination. And the less you get caught with your pants down, the less bare surface area you'll be exposing to the elements.

The same obviously goes for bowel movements. You have some control here, too, believe it or not. The solution involves "acclimation." When the deer season rolls around, most hunters are not accustomed to the early hours required for reaching their stands by sunrise. Consequently, their digestive systems are out of whack. But by keeping earlier hours *before* the season, bodily

To make sure that you're in top form when a buck like this steps out from behind a tree, eat properly and get into good physical shape before the season begins.

functions can be put into line so that elimination can be accomplished before climbing that stand.

Dr. Pozos added that the body's defensive strategy against the cold can be acclimated, too. By purposely underdressing before the season and then spending time in the woods, you can prepare other bodily functions—including metabolism and the respiratory system. This way, when the first wintry cold front hits, it won't seem like a frigid January storm. A recent poll, in fact, somewhat confirmed Pozo's claim that the human body can acclimitize to the weather conditions. Respondents were asked which was the "mildest" month, November or March. Nearly 80 percent of the participants said that March was milder. In most of the states where the interviews were conducted, however, November had a higher mean temperature. What's going on here is acclimation: by the time March arrives, the body has become conditioned by previous winter months.

All of this goes to show that there is a lot more to stand hunting than simply finding a good location. After strategies have been drawn, go ahead and climb that stand, keeping these ideas in mind. And stick to it. You *can* stand it.

10

The World's
Best Bowhunter

One hunter in particular who can stand it is Myles Keller, arguably one of the world's best bowhunters. And the reason that Keller can stand it is because he has worked hard to get trophy whitetail hunting down to a science. This is a man who makes few mistakes, and you can bet that when he chooses a place to sit, that spot will most often produce a big buck.

For most deer hunters, especially bow hunters, luck plays a mighty big role in determining the outcome of each season. You know, being in the right place at the right time and all that jazz. But not for Myles Keller.

Come on, you say, a guy who's arrowed more than 20 Pope & Young whitetail bucks—more than anyone else in the world—must have had a few lucky days behind him. And what about those record-book black bears? You mean to say that there isn't a close-shave story there, either?

Nope. Dull hunts. Boring shots. All of them.

But this guy, Myles Keller, he's quite a story. Nothing mundane about his whitetail knowledge and the strategies that he has refined over the years from successful hunts. He's got his tactics down pat—to the point that, when he sets up for a particular buck and finally makes his move, it'll be history for another trophy deer.

How does he do it? You can't put it into a 25-words-or-less

capsule, but by taking a close look at each component of his techniques, you'll get a good feel for what true trophy deer hunting is all about.

Myles Keller is not interested in anything unless it has a direct bearing on mature, large-racked bucks. Of course, that really narrows the field down, yet he somehow manages to pull it off every year.

And he does it just about every place he hunts. He does it elk hunting out west (his Pope & Young bull was the best taken in the entire state of Colorado that year for both the gun and the bow season); he does it whitetail hunting in Wisconsin (his big eight-pointer scored a whopping 175⅝ inches); and he does it black bear hunting in Minnesota (a 510-pound, 21⁴⁄₁₆ Pope & Young bruin). He has also placed whitetails in the books from Michigan and Missouri.

But like I said, his actual hunts are pretty boring. He doesn't go near selected ambush sites until he's confident that everything is just right. It may take a week, a month or a season to get to that point, but he seems to get there like clockwork.

It's hard to believe that a man who has amassed such an unprecedented record almost quit bowhunting altogether before he fulfilled his destiny as one of the world's greatest deer hunters. As a young teenager, he walked to the headquarters of Herters, the once-famous sporting goods mail-order houses, to buy his first bow. On the way home on that same day, he shot his first deer, a doe feeding at the edge of a field.

An eight-pointer was his next target, but a misplaced shot—high and toward the stomach area—taught Keller the necessity of clean kills in the sport of bowhunting. When he couldn't find the deer despite hours of searching, he went back to the farm to tell his father that he wasn't ever going to hunt deer with a bow again. The thought of losing such a beautiful animal was more than he could bear.

But the next morning, he had a change of heart. Aided by his father's sharp eye, they found the deer—less than 100 yards from where the shot was made. The arrow somehow made its way into the artery just below the backbone, and the deer bled to death within minutes. Later, the young Keller learned that one of the bow's limbs was badly twisted; it was a wonder that he had hit the deer at all.

Despite his travels, Myles Keller does 80 percent of his bowhunting within a 10-mile radius of his home. It is, indeed, a

Myles Keller has about two dozen big bucks like this in his trophy collection. He's a hunter who goes "for big bucks only."

worthwhile area for a serious bowhunter who intends to consistently score on trophy-class bucks; rich farm soils laced with lush river bottoms are the perfect complement to a decent gene pool of high-racked bucks. But Keller by no means considers this holy ground for record-bound deer.

"There are a lot more big bucks out there than the average hunter thinks," he said. "The trouble is, hunters seldom give the mature bucks credit; if a guy shoots a 1½- or 2½-year-old deer, he starts thinking that all the rest of the bucks act or react the same way. Bucks old enough to grow a large set of antlers are wise to the day-in and day-out ploys of most hunters."

Keller feels that modern deer hunting is approached much like a man punching in at work—you just put in your time and, sooner or later, the bonuses will come. Keller does just the opposite. He never goes near a selected site unless he's absolutely sure that the buck he's after will be "working his route" in an *unalarmed* manner.

"I don't like to hunt escape-route bucks," he told me. "It's hard enough to fool a buck on even terms, let alone one that's on edge and working his senses overtime."

What's wrong with a little Russian roulette on a deer stand? Plenty, according to Keller. On rare occasion, you may by chance intercept a nice buck but, almost always, the buck will wind you and you'll probably never know that he exists. This becomes part of the vicious cycle that reinforces the notion that there aren't any big bucks in your area.

To get around this, Keller scouts the area until he knows the buck's home territory completely.

"I never stop scouting," he explained. "Whether it's a trip to the grocery store or out on the grader plowing a county road, I'm looking for tracks and racks."

And he looks for something that most bowhunters never consider, something he calls "the big picture." Instead of keying in on a particular runway that a buck is most likely to use, he first tries to establish a buck's routine. Without doing this, finding the weak point in a buck's travels could not be accomplished. Typically, a mature animal travels the safest routes, where it can rely on its keen senses to keep out of danger. Putting yourself on equal footing with those senses is useless, Keller insists, but find the one part of a buck's pattern where he isn't using his senses to full advantage, and you'll quickly gain the upper hand. That's basically how Keller outwits trophy bucks.

Rather than keying in on one runway, Keller looks at "the big picture." Within that big picture is usually one place where the buck is not using his senses to full advantage. That is the buck's weak spot. And that is how Myles Keller outwits trophy bucks.

"There are no shortcuts to trophy deer," he said. "But they all make mistakes eventually. It's up to the hunter to predict the mistakes before they happen and to be ready when the opportunity presents itself."

The story of how he took a Pope & Young buck illustrates this point perfectly. By putting together the deer's overall routine, Keller was able to determine that each morning the buck would head out of a breeding area and follow a ditch bank toward a 10-acre woodlot. The buck would circle the entire woodlot before entering to bed down for the day. Just before the big buck got to the woodlot, however, he would feel relatively confident and would cut the corner from where the ditch ran by the woods. At this point, the deer would also be quartering against the wind. Keller reasoned that, if he approached this spot from the opposite side of the tree line and positioned himself in exactly the right place, the buck would not be able to wind him while he was cutting the corner. Keller's reasoning resulted in a 15-yard shot and a Pope & Young buck.

One of Keller's favorite ways to figure out the big picture is by posting on a fenceline. These are obvious travel routes leading to and from bedding and feeding areas, and they afford the added benefit of openness—you can see for miles, in many instances. Keller spends countless hours waiting and observing deer from fencelines.

"To me, a fenceline is like a window to a buck's living room," he said. "I can look in without being detected and get a good feel for where the kitchen and bedroom are. And I can do all this without going in and disturbing a thing."

But don't get the idea that all Keller does is lounge around while glassing deer from a distance. He cuts no corners to "set up" over a buck's apparent Achilles' heel. On a normal year's hunt, he's usually got at least a dozen or more stands carefully erected at locations that he knows could produce a trophy buck. The real trick is choosing the right one. And should he make a mistake so that a buck picks him up, he'll yank that stand out and completely relocate it, provided he finds another weak link for another set up. And after the move, he won't touch the new stand for at least a few more days, even if he moves it only 20 yards.

Over the years, a number of reliable setup areas have emerged from Keller's copious field notes and observations. One such pet place is what he calls perimeter trails.

"Bucks—really big bucks—don't normally travel along the

One of Keller's favorite ways to see the big picture is to post on a fenceline. "A fenceline is like a window to a buck's living room," he says. From a fenceline you can observe the buck, like this one moving from his bedding to feeding area, in his daily routine without being detected.

same trails as does and immature bucks," he said. "I've found that they use their own travel lines off the well-beaten paths, instead. Of course, a lot depends on the terrain. In farm country that's broken up by woodlots and creek bottoms, bucks will often utilize perimeter trails that skirt the edge of heavier cover."

Keller has shot a number of dandy bucks off perimeter trails for the simple reason that these routes often lead deer along a route—even if it's for a short distance—where they can't use their nose. The irony here is that perimeter trails exist because a buck has walked the woodlot, scent-checking for danger before deciding that the area is safe for spending the day. Again, by utilizing the wind at the precise place for his stand, Keller can intercept unsuspecting bucks.

This setup can be worked two ways. First, deer coming out to feed in fields at the end of the day can be seen before last light, whereas the hunter who watches over the actual field edge will be lucky to see fawns and yearlings. And second, the tactic works on deer coming out of the fields in the morning, looking for a safe place to hide out for the day. Earlier in the year, prior to heavy rutting activity, Keller feels that perimeter trails, when properly understood, can be very productive.

But given a choice, Keller, like most bowhunters, would much rather hunt during the rut. It's a time when he goes all out, squeezing as much energy as he can from his body. But unlike many other hunters, he does not hunt over primary scrapes. Instead, he uses them to find short travel routes where a buck is likely to take a chance for a short distance, rely on his eyes and not on his nose and travel crosswind. Bucks that have been chasing does all night are often in a hurry to bed down, and a wise hunter can often pull this one off.

"This is the best and only reliable way to get a big buck," he explained. "Besides being preoccupied with the sex urge, bucks are on the move a lot more than at any other time, so it really increases your chances."

The way Keller uses scrapes to his advantage is a trick that works equally well for farm country bucks and deep woods deer. Most hunters would like to believe that bucks check their scrapes during the daylight hours, freshening them often. Keller doesn't buy that for trophy animals. Invariably, an older buck will scent-check his scrapes from downwind; in the process, most hunters are detected and easily avoided. So, what to do? Simple.

"Bucks—really big bucks—don't normally travel along the same trails as does and immature bucks," Keller says. "I've found that they use their own travel lines off the well-beaten paths, instead." According to Keller big bucks in farm country use perimeter trails that skirt the edge of heavier cover. That's where he bagged this nice buck.

Figure out how the buck approaches his scenting route and set up downwind—or preferably crosswind—from that.

"I find that bucks usually check their scrapes at a distance of about 70 yards or so," he said. "I start there and work my way back around from the primary breeding areas."

By "primary breeding areas" Keller means only those scrapes that are really torn up, with numerous trails coming in and going out of them. They're a far cry from the isolated scrape made here or there on impulse by a lesser buck.

All of the scouting and all of the whitetail wisdom in the world is useless if a deer is able to get his nose on you. Nothing is more important to Keller than beating a buck's sniffer.

"That's the name of the game," he often says. "Bucks in more open edge country rely totally on their sense of smell; it never lets them down. But if you use your head the way a whitetail uses its nose, you're off to a good start."

The rituals that Keller routinely goes through to counteract his own body odor sounds almost kinky. First, he washes all his hunting clothes (most hunters forget the underwear) in baking soda, using a box or so for one wash. Then he air dries them. And he never wears them around the house or camp where they could pick up undesirable odors; the minute he's done hunting, off they go. He stores them with a branch of a tree native to the area that he's hunting.

He also cakes his own body with baking soda and whenever he's near water he plunges in no matter what the temperature. A clean body is essential, he insists; most hunters would agree. But he has one ritual that tops them all.

"I don't know if you should print this—some people might think I'm weird," he told me. "But when I'm really serious, I put a plastic bag over my head (snugged over the top of his head down to his eyebrows)—you know, the lunch-bag size. Then I put on a fresh stocking cap—one that's heavily laden with baking soda."

Indeed, it sounds weird, but when he explains his line of reasoning, it seems to make sense: If most of the body's heat escapes through the head, then a lot of scent must also rise from that area, as well. By keeping a lid on it, so to speak, you can cut down on the amount of scent released, as well.

Keller takes other precautions that he considers mandatory. For one thing, he frequently hunts while wearing rubber waders because he knows from trapping that leather boots leave a scent trail behind in the woods. Whenever he climbs one of his tree

Keller believes that older bucks scent-check their scrapes from downwind. In the process, he says, a hunter hunting close to the scrape will be detected by the buck and easily avoided.

stands, he dons a pair of surgical gloves. On stand, he does not sit atop a platform with an old piece of carpeting—that's like putting a big scent vent of human odors up in a tree, he explained. Instead, he'll make sure that the scrap piece of rug has been thoroughly washed—again, in baking soda—and hung in the breeze to dry. What's more, he never affixes it to the platform with any smelly glues. By keeping a plastic garbage bag snugged over it when the stand is not in use, he avoids noise problems when it freezes up. He simply removes the garbage bag with any built up snow and ice and is then able to sit or stand as quietly and as odorlessly as possible.

Most commercially made scents are ineffective, according to Keller, especially the so-called doe mating lures.

Keller uses fox urine and a couple of homemade concoctions that help to confuse deer about his ground scent, but he doesn't think anything can actually mask human odor. The only line of defense is to avoid sweating, keep immaculately clean, have plenty of changes of hunting clothing and stay out of a buck's area until it's time for the kill.

Although most of Keller's trophies have been arrowed from a stand, as hunter pressure grows, stalking becomes an increasingly important tool in his repertoire. A deadly method is to stalk bedding bucks lying in small depressions among farm crops. Cornfields, especially, lend themselves to this approach. Keller believes that stalking takes a little nerve but, more importantly, time.

One fall afternoon, he spotted a huge buck feeding on the periphery of a field of standing corn. It was already getting late, but the wind was right. Unfortunately, the ground was frozen and very crunchy, so he had to remove his boots and walk in his socks in order to avoid spooking the buck. He came to within 50 yards before he ran out of time—shooting light had finally vanished. His feet were almost frostbitten.

With all those records to his credit, and a system that appears unbeatable, what's next for Myles Keller?

When I asked him, he just smiled and said, "Probably more rewarding hunts." But then he gave me a funny look. "You know," he added, "I feel like a bum for even saying this—lots of guys are always saying this—but there's a buck just a few miles from my house that could be the next typical world record. His last upward point is six or seven inches, and he's got six perfect tines to each side, plus mass and a tall, wide rack. I've seen him several times, and he'll go at least 190. That's what I'll be up to very soon."

11

Musical Chairs
For Big Bucks

But what about those of us who aren't Myles Keller. Some of us simply hunt in country where the traditional methods don't work like they're supposed to. What are we supposed to do to tag those trophy bucks we just know are dying of old age right under our noses?

I pondered this question as I was camped in front of the fire one crisp October night, watching the logs burn down. As the flames darted before me, I mulled over the shortcomings of all the techniques we've used on deer at our camp. The methods were far from flawless and the country we hunt really brings that out.

Our camp is located in northern Minnesota, where all the eye can see for miles on end are tag alder thickets interrupted only by an occasional aspen stand. A few conifers compete for some sunlight but the high water table and clay soils do not favor evergreens. To make matters worse, the topography is as flat as a crew cut. Also, because there are no bottlenecks, you can never be sure where the deer are likely to cross.

Selecting a productive tree stand is more like playing Russian roulette than doing intelligent field reconnaissance. On top of this, the deer bed, feed and breed all in the same general area. If you try to move in on them they'll pick up your movements and just slide over to the next thicket.

What about deer drives? They're like trying to eat soup with a fork. The deer will run you ragged with their double-dealing, double-backing tactics. I can never forget the time a group of hunters invaded our territory and put on a big deer drive right through the heart of our main hunting area. They came from farm country farther south and thought it would be a snap to herd the deer toward their blockers. I could hear them coming long before I saw them, as they yapped and howled like a pack of coon hounds. Instinctively, I braced myself for the possibility of a buck being pushed my way.

Their calling drew louder and louder—my finger was on the safety when I heard some crashing in the brush near the sight lane to my left. Suddenly, a heavy-set fellow wearing a faded pink sweatshirt popped out into view and, without noticing me, let out another one of his patented yip-yip-yeows. I relaxed and poured a cup of mushroom soup from my Thermos, as the big fellow sauntered past my stand.

So much for deer drives, I scoffed silently, as I turned back to my sight lines. And what do you suppose I saw, not more than 30 yards away? Yup. A beautiful buck. But don't ask how many points—it was the last thing on earth I expected to see, and I must have startled it just as it startled me. In a flick of an eyelash it whirled and bounded off, leaving me gawking in disbelief. Now, I'm always ready for a double-backing buck.

If the deer are so hard to pinpoint, why don't we do a lot of stillhunting? Well, we've had some limited success with tiptoeing between the thickets but, for the most part, it's so thick that just about every two-legged animal ends up using the same basic routes. It doesn't take long for the critters to wise up and avoid those corridors.

Yea, this is miserable country to hunt deer, I thought. Yet I thanked God for it. After all, any country to hunt deer is better than no country at all. And though I didn't come up with any answers that night, I realized that I am lucky enough to hunt with an enterprising group of hunters who have refused to give in to the elements and bow to tradition. And by so doing, we've turned a hopeless situation into one in which we've got the best of the three worlds.

By first dealing with the inadequacies of each of the three traditional techniques, and then focusing on each one's strengths, we've synthesized a perfect strategy to fit our unique situation. It wasn't exactly an instant hit but, by working together, my buddies and I have been able to improvise and combine all three

The author's musical chairs technique can push a big buck, like this one sneaking around the hunter, past a fellow musical chairs hunter.

approaches. After a short, but exasperating trial-and-error period, we've come up with a system that is almost foolproof and relatively easy to pull off—our musical chairs system. And it should work anywhere that three or more hunters are willing to combine their efforts with some dedication and forethought.

Its overall effectiveness is due to its ultra-flexibility: When deer appear to be on the move, we can wait them out; when they are bedded down, we can often coax them to move in a controlled direction; and if deer numbers are down in a given area, or there are too many hunters, we can move into a new area.

The heart of this system is the careful selection of several deer stand sites. We scout the area out as thoroughly as time permits, but we don't need to know as much about deer behavior in a given area as the typical stand hunter does. Final pieces to the puzzle will eventually fall into place because our method provides the details. Once the high-percentage locations are set, such as swamp edges, openings between thickets and trails downwind from scrapes, we take into account backup sites for differing wind conditions. Naturally, you must be downwind from where you expect to sight deer, and that could be 50 yards this way or that, depending upon the wind quadrant.

Next you need a game plan. It should be flexible because few days are duplicates of one another. The most important aspect of your strategy is commitment. Every member absolutely must stick to predetermined ''rules'' for the day, whether he likes it or not. Keep in mind that you can always make changes the following time out—provided the whole group goes along with it.

Finally, you need at least three hunters. As many as eight will work, and four or five is ideal.

By now you should really be catching on. In a nutshell, what we do is trade deer stands—musical chairs style. We coordinate our movements, however, right down to the second, and each guy knows exactly where everyone else is, where they are going and about when they're going to get there. Many bucks are bagged off the stands, of course, but the success rate is surprisingly decent for guys who are moseying from one stand to the next.

A typical maneuver involving three hunters goes something like this. We set our watches to the second as we leave the shack, which is easy to do with digital watches nowadays, and we agree to a time schedule and direction pattern. Our stands will punctuate the terrain in more of a circle than a straight line, so we can cover more ground and are more likely to hem deer in rather than move them out of the general area.

Picture one hunter at the noon position of a clock, another at 4 o'clock and one at 8 o'clock. At 10:00 a.m., the hunter at the noon position heads in a clockwise direction for the 4 o'clock position. After he arrives, the hunter at 4 o'clock then stillhunts his way to the hunter at 8 o'clock who, in turn, works his way to the noon position.

The direction hunters move depends upon the wind. They could have chosen, for instance, to go in a counter-clockwise direction. The main idea here is to maximize everyone's chances, realizing that it is unavoidable for some individuals at one time or another to be moving with the wind. By sketching stand locations and wind direction on a topographic map, you can get a good idea which way is the most advantageous for the group as a whole. To best do this, have the map blown up so that a one-mile section is about the size of a normal 8½- x 11-inch piece of paper.

Another good idea is to avoid too much traipsing in the interior sector of your area. Due to topographic and vegetative constraints, it is not possible to make a direct beeline for the next stand. And you wouldn't really want to, either. While stillhunting in between, it makes more sense to probe those areas that might hold a bedding buck rather than taking the path of least resistance out in more open country. But when you do it, make your meanderings spiral to the outside, as opposed to the inside, of your route. With only three guys you can't cover a very large area, and you could end up spooking the deer out of the immediate vicinity.

With more hunters you have more options. Say you have a party of eight. That's enough guys to cover two or three square miles. In this instance, you could switch stands by two's or work them in two separate circles, one going clockwise, the other going counter-clockwise. It all depends on the terrain and how deer react when you move them off their beds.

Here's one example of how one group, hunting along a river bottom or creek bed, might improvise. Let's assume the valley runs north/south.

Stands could be aligned like a tic-tac-toe grid, with the middle square unoccupied. That way sentinels could cover the edge of the ridge—where deer often establish well-worn runways—and both the head and tail of the bottomland. With this arrangement, you'd be better off sending hunters cross-wind through the valley. And two at a time paralleling one another might be better than singles, to take advantage of deer trying to circle back rather than moving across to the other side.

How to handle each end of the draw depends on a number of factors. Are there beaver ponds or other such bottlenecks? How about narrow necks? This is a key position that should see a lot of activity, so it is doubly important to man it with a constant watchful eye, keeping it plugged for deer escaping to the north or south.

But that shouldn't be a problem with the musical chairs system. Even though the average adult attention span is only 20 minutes or so, boredom will seldom be a problem. By rotating stands—typically on a two-hour basis for slack periods of the day—each hunter gets to see a change in scenery and his senses are always keen. And if staying warm has been a problem, there's good news on that front, too. Just as your toes begin to numb it will be time to hop down and sneak over to the next stand. Your circulation will kick in and you'll literally be pumped up for the next vigil.

Because an entire day won't be spent in the same spot, elaborate permanent stands aren't necessary. Lightweight, portable tree stands, made mostly of aluminum, and a set of tree climbers have become standard equipment for us. With them we get up a considerable distance for a good vantage point (be sure to check state laws for height restrictions), and keep our scent off the ground below us. And if we find deer to be skirting around us, we can tailor our alterations to suit our needs.

One need that cannot be altered, however, is for each member of the musical chairs serenade to know the lay of the land well enough to locate each stand. If anyone is shaky on this point, he'd better not participate in the rotation; he could single-handedly throw off the timing of the maneuver and ruin everyone's hunt for the day. Every time I think of this prerequisite, I remember a guy from another party who got lost and showed up at one of my stands.

"Have you seen Ralph?" he asked.

"Who's Ralph?" I replied.

At that, he turned white, spun on his heels and promptly began yelling and cussing for Ralph, as he barreled through the woods. I sure hope Ralph got what he deserved.

After a half dozen seasons with musical chairs, I feel that I've learned more about deer behavior than by 20 years of ordinary stand hunting.

Deer pull a Houdini act and seem to disappear soon after the season's first few shots, the author says. Only by sticking to the musical chairs system has his party been able to keep up with the deer.

One question that begs for an answer is, "Where do all the deer go after the first day of the season?" Some say they head deeper into the woods. Others insist that deer, especially big bucks, become strictly nocturnal and bed out of sight during the day. Still others argue that swamps and tangled thickets—which two-legged predators avoid—are favored hideouts.

Who knows? Until I radio-collar a couple hundred bucks, I'm not going to hazard a guess. All I know is that deer pull a Houdini act in my area and seem to disappear without warning soon after the first few shots ring out. Only by sticking to the musical chairs system has my party been able to keep up with the deer. One thing is certain: deer do alter their routes, and anyone stuck in just one place could be in for a long wait.

Musical chairs hunting also helps you cope with hunter pressure, which used to scare the tar out of me because I'd been rooked out of more than one big buck by an intruder at the last moment. Here is a case in point:

On opening day, the guys in my party set up for an all day vigil without exchanging stands. From previous openers and last-minute scouting efforts, we had a pretty good idea of what the first morning onslaught was likely to be. We knew, for instance, that an army of weekend whiskey drinkers was going to drive the river bottom to the west, and that the deer camp to the east of us would hunt as close to us as they dare. But what we didn't know, on this particular morning, was that a new wave of three-wheeling gangsters would move into our area from the north. Jim Stocco, our self-appointed leader for the day, showed up at my stand at 10 o'clock wearing a long face.

"We gotta move," he said. "Those buzzards on the three-wheelers are scaring all the deer south."

"But there's nothing but that big alder pocket worth hunting," I protested. "And we haven't pruned back our sight lines there for at least four years."

"You got a better idea?" he asked. "You know the deer are in there...and we know how to move them, don't we?"

Stocco was right. After regrouping at the shack, we headed for the snarled alder swamp and set up at our old stand locations. Sure, it was thick. Our cuttings were so grown over that we had very few shooting lanes. But it was also thick with deer—I shagged two out on the way in to my stand at high noon. It was just a matter of sticking to our game plan.

The final tally for the day was impressive, considering how

The author caught this buck trying to sneak around drivers in another hunting party that tried to push deer straight ahead to standers. Bucks like this are often more likely to double back.

bleak it started out: two bucks, an eight-pointer and a forkhorn, were hanging on the meat pole that evening. One was drilled about 10 minutes after I had nestled into my stand (perhaps it was one of the two deer I caught a glimpse of on the way in) and the other was shot by Stocco as he threaded his way from his stand to mine.

With a little imagination, group hunting by musical chairs can work in your area and put meat in the pot. Swapping stands is a fun way to outsmart whitetails. But don't expect everyone to embrace it with open arms. In my camp, four of us work with the system and two don't. The telling statistic is, however, who shoots the most deer.

To date, those that are "musically inclined" are outdoing the "stand deaf" by a whopping six to one margin.

So don't be discouraged if the results on your first attempts aren't perfect. On my trial run I felt almost as silly as when I first tried rattling up a buck. At one point, two of us were exchanging sheepish faces at the base of one of our tree stands when a deer suddenly bolted less than 10 paces away. Then there was the time when two of the guys showed up at the same time...at the wrong stand.

Oh well. We stuck to it, and I'm glad we did.

12

Deer:
Weather Or Not

By virtue of the technique itself, musical chairs is a method by which the hunter switches stands during the course of the day's hunt. But switching stands shouldn't be a practice exercised only by those employing this tactic. Other factors should influence stand selection on a particular hunt. And one of the major factors would be the weather.

On the eve of one firearms deer season, I was preaching my annual deer sermon to my teenaged nephew. Learning the secret of flexibility, I said, is better than being lucky. I told him that because I knew the kid thought he had the hottest stand area in the deep woods, and I didn't want him to fritter away the whole deer season on just one spot, much less one tactic.

So what did I do when—get this—50 mile-an-hour gales the next morning pushed over puny popple trees like they were sticks of straw? Like an old fuddy-duddy, I stayed on my stand. All day. And I didn't see much, except for a small spike on the tail of a leading doe, who looked like she had just seen a hundred ghosts. I made the same crucial mistake a lot of hunters make—I failed to take the weather into account when considering my strategy for the day. And I knew better.

I've said it many times before, and I'll say it again (with a promise to listen to myself from now on): Local weather patterns can affect your deer hunt as much as the rut and hunter pressure—the two most popular conversation pieces in most hunting circles today. Show me a hunter who bags a good buck year after year, and I'll show you a guy who listens to weather forecasts like they're directions to a pirate's treasure chest. The discriminating nimrod learns the basic principles of how deer react to varying climactic conditions—wind, rain, fog, snow—and adjusts his daily tactics accordingly. That's all there is to it.

But are deer really that sensitive to weather changes? And if so, how can one predict changes to their movement patterns before they happen? Research, coupled with experience, indicates that severe changes in the weather, particularly if two forces are interacting with one another, such as wind and rain, do affect where deer tend to go and what they'll do. Like many deer fanatics, I've been fascinated by this phenomenon. Only in recent years, however, have I incorporated it into my in-the-field tactics. Since then, I haven't been praying for "good" weather; I make the necessary adjustment(s) and roll with the punches.

Rain, like it or not, is one element with which every hunter must contend. How it impacts deer, though, depends on how intense it is and its duration. Deer all but ignore light to moderate rains, as they go about their daily business. But extended periods of precipitation add subtle modifications to the time periods deer actively feed.

I remember one fall, during the bow season, when it rained every day for two weeks. During this wet stretch, I learned an interesting lesson from Dave Hudacek, a bowhunter from Superior, Wisconsin. He had let the weather put a damper on his outlook and he had gotten a little lazy. As a result, he missed out on a good opportunity for a particular buck that had been monitoring a field edge and lagging behind does that would come out to feed on alfalfa after dusk.

Toward the end of the week, after seeing little encouraging activity, Hudacek decided to check the field for tracks. Perhaps the deer were using another field, he thought. Much to his amazement, the area was littered with prints, large and small. How could that be? He had stayed there well past sunset several evenings in a row without sighting a single animal. They had to be coming out late at night, he concluded. As he trudged back to the truck, he could see tractor lights coming his way. It was the farmer who owned the fields he had been hunting for several years.

"Where have you been?" the usually stoic farmer asked, with an uncharacteristic excitement to his voice. "That good buck

The discriminating nimrod knows the basic principles of how deer react to varying climatic conditions—wind, rain, fog, snow—and adjusts his daily tactics accordingly. In this chapter the author shows you how.

you've been dogging is back again this year, and he's a dandy.''

"You mean you've seen him?'' Dave asked.

"Seen him!? Why, he's been in the east field every afternoon for nearly a week.''

"Oh yea?'' Dave questioned, not knowing if the farmer was kidding or not. "And I suppose he shows up early and leaves early, say, by 3:30 or 4:00 o'clock.''

"Exactly,'' the farmer responded, somewhat puzzled. "Just like clockwork...''

It was a tough lesson, but Hudacek learned it. The very next day he came very close to taking the biggest field buck he'd ever seen.

What was happening was a common occurrence worth remembering. The deer had adjusted their feeding schedules according to the light. Skies had been dark and overcast for so long that the deer took advantage of it and fed during afternoon hours, rather than at night, when it was really dark (it had been a new moon period). They could do this despite the fact that the bow season was in full swing because the rain had discouraged every other hunter in the area from venturing out.

Rain mixed with fog does a similar thing to deer. They tend to roam about in open country with even more recklessness. Of course, if you've got a stand back in the thick stuff, it could be a long wait. Obviously, the thing to do is move out toward the openings if you hunt deep woods, and move in closer to the croplands if you hunt farm country. Stands situated along runways leading to these feeding areas are unbeatable.

But the stillhunter who has enough patience to sneak along at a crippled snail's pace has a couple of advantages over the stand hunter, under these circumstances. For one, he'll be able to scour those areas that could never be approached under normal, dry conditions. Certain areas along riverbottoms, where big bucks bed and feed intermittently come to mind. So do the thickets with small openings where truly monster bucks only venture from at night. And if your confidence level is low when it comes to stillhunting, give it a serious effort when the woods are wet. You can get away with murder, compared to those times when leaves and twigs underfoot pop like Rice Krispies on a TV commercial. All it takes is one positive memory to erase the stigma that says deer can only be bagged from a stand.

What about storms—when rains pound the earth on the heels of high winds? Then what? Well, your tactics must change because

Hunting from a stand during clear, calm days may be just the ticket. But when the weather turns nasty, this technique will often prove fruitless. Instead, hop off the stand and poke around the edges of swamps and pockets of brush. During a storm a deer's senses will be impaired.

the deer's reactions to sounds will be completely different. It will not only be miserable out there, but the woods will be smitten with wild and confusing noises. During a storm a deer's vision and hearing will be impaired. Worst of all, a deer's trusty nose will be unreliable at detecting danger because winds will swirl from every quadrant and scent tends to stick to the falling precipitation. You can bet the grocery money that every deer in the country is going to be holed up in the thickest, safest clump of real estate imaginable. And they'll stay put as long as it takes to wait out the storm.

Naturally, sitting on a stand is a waste of time. Instead, you've got to go to the deer, for they surely won't be coming to you. Poking around from thicket to thicket along the edges of cedar swamps, alder brush pockets and hemlocks is a good idea for the hunter going solo. In farm country, don't leave a single cattail swamp unchecked, especially ones with some high ground within.

A more effective method would be small, controlled drives of the two-man or four-man variety. Two advantages await the drivers under these conditions. First, the drivers themselves are almost as likely as the blockers to get a close shot at a standing or circling animal. Second, once a buck holes up in one of these areas, he's very reluctant to leave—like a pheasant or grouse burrowed under a small snow drift—and you have to almost kick him out.

Another successful technique is to hunt the open fields. Minutes after a long, intense storm, does will move into the fields to feed. Bucks, meanwhile, will have also been holed up during the storm. If you're lucky enough to come across this situation during the rut, you'll find that the bucks won't wait for the cover of darkness to move into the open field and court the does. If you hunt open farm country, glassing field edges and river bottoms from fencelines and roadways should pay off. Try to get the overall picture of deer movement patterns in relation to the wind before trying to set up.

For deep woods hunters, I know no better method than to sit-and-sneak along the edges of different cover types. For instance, where mast crops are prevalent, slowly work the fingers of the oaks, particularly where they reach out and drop into thick bottomlands. Take your time and be sure to sit over the best looking spots for at least 20 minutes, better yet, an hour.

One time I found myself sneaking along a Christmas tree pine plantation after a big front passed through the area. Dark, billowing clouds had dumped three inches of rain in just the last hour, and over 10 inches saturated the ground from the previous

Snowstorms later in the season affect deer much differently. Small drives in thickets will be your best choice if you hunt in a party.

night. I wasn't really expecting to see a deer, just some sign that might give me a clue or two. As I rounded the northeast corner of the 40-acre patch, two bucks bolted almost from under my feet. Had I been able to maintain any degree of composure, I'm sure I could have picked my shot with plenty of time to spare. I just didn't expect to bump into anything out in the open like that so soon after a severe storm. From now on, you can bet I'll be prepared. It's another one of those nuggets of truth worth remembering.

Snow can have a profound effect on deer behavior, varying from all but depositing a good buck in your lap, to making it miserable and next to impossible to get close to a deer. Tracker Noble Carlson, of course, always prays for snow, but he will be the first to admit that just as no two snow crystals are alike, no two snowfalls affect deer movements the same way.

"The first two snowfalls of the year are always the best," he says. "That's when I can pretty much guarantee a younger buck, say, 200 pounds, for the meat pole. And if I find the set of an older, bigger one—closer to 250 pounds—I can almost guarantee that, too."

For anyone else, such a statement would be little more than bragging. But for Noble, it's a statement of fact.

"What makes it close to a sure bet," Noble explained to me, "is the fact that the dang deer think they're safe. They think they still blend in with the surroundings, like they did before the snow hit. But in reality, their big brown coats are easy to spot once you get familiar with what to look for and how to do it. And another thing, the does and spikes kind of romp around between bedding and feeding stints, instead of going straight from one area to the next."

But it's important to remember, too, that *you* show up quite well in the white stuff, and because deer also know that snow muffles every sound, they will turn to their eyes to help them confirm their noses' suspicions. Smart hunters don a pair of binoculars at this time—compacts in the deep woods and more powerful optics in farm country—to aid in viewing from afar. You'll appreciate the way snow reflects light and gives you added resolution and detail, even in dim situations.

Snowstorms later in the season affect deer much differently. The temperatures will be colder, and often there will be a crunchy crust associated with it—if not beneath it, certainly on top of it. It's a good time to check out the thickets again. Deer will need to conserve heat and energy, and any place out of the wind where cedars, hemlocks or black spruce can obstruct nagging northwest or northeast winds is a good bet. Again, small drives are your best choice if you hunt in a party. A lot of ground can be covered in a day, and the deer will hear the drivers coming from a good distance; standers should take this into account and be very careful about approaching the exits of the thicket they intend to block.

Stand hunters are at a decided disadvantage if their location is one picked while scouting on a balmy October afternoon. But stand hunting should not be ruled out entirely when a snowstorm hits, if the sites are selected from previous experiences in the area while the snow was flying. Deer often use the same hold-outs year after year, and if it is in an area of heavy snowfall, they will yard up in those traditional grounds generation after generation.

This late season is also a high percentage time to look for a heavy-racked buck. With the hype of the rut behind him, an old buck will, for the first time, begin to seriously think about food. Low-growing browse interspersed within the thickets are prime spots. Crops close to swamps and riverbottoms get the nod in farmlands. If the area is small and isolated, try a portable tree stand and sit it out. Eventually a buck should show up. But if it's a larger area, I favor the sit-and-sneak method, at least until I narrow down preferred hiding/feeding areas.

And what about hunting in the thick of a snowstorm? Standard whitetail dogma dictates that deer sit tight, as should you, until the front passes through. I wholeheartedly disagree. Sure the deer hunker down, but that can be to your advantage if you get off your stand.

The only percentage shot for sneaking up on a wary bedded buck is when it's snowing sideways. He'll have a heck of a time seeing or hearing you. The main obstacles are making sure you see antlers, and getting off a quick shot. Of course, it won't be "easy." What might stack the odds in your favor, though, is first knowing where the bedding areas are, so you can keep up your concentration without wavering—a must for this nerve-racking affair.

And what about before the coming of the snow or the rains? Well, every dedicated outdoorsman knows that wild game becomes active just prior to a falling barometer and that it's a good time to be on stand where deer cross regularly. But knowing what the weather is going to be like before it hits is the key to drawing up the best strategy for any day's hunt. Therefore, always have

The Best Tactics
During The Worst Weather

Weather Type	Where to Hunt	How to Hunt
Early snow	Small openings, especially the edges	With expectancy! Deer move a lot; trails, tracking
Late snow	Low, dense thickets, maybe in vicinity of established deer yards; pines, hemlocks, cedars	Drive smaller thickets, sneak alone or just poke around; especially looking for bedded bucks in the thick of the storm
Heavy rain with strong winds	Edges of thick cover —deer use their eyes more than usual; most active midday	Have a stand on a major travel route (with a roof or umbrella); two-man sneaks, also
Light rain, steady wind	Trails between bedding and feeding areas; openings within thickets	Stillhunting; tree stands
Periods of extended rain	Beds in dense cover, typically with overhead cover	Stillhunt the bedding areas
Storm, just prior	Feeding areas; runways leading to food sources	On a stand
Storm, just after	Food sources, especially in areas low in hunter pressure	Sit-and-move method, if not sure of exact spot(s)
Fog	Clearing edges, crop land strips	Stillhunt; glance ahead, if possible
Bitter cold	Lowlands; dips in hardwood ridges; pine plantations	Stick to thickets and wind-break areas

Deer's Reactions	Comments
Feel confident; some even romp and "play"	Don't miss this opportunity—take vacation time, if possible; deer really stick out, but they think they're still well-camouflaged
Wait for snows to subside because of difficulty of movement; may feed at midday	Not bad time to nail a trophy; big bucks start thinking about food instead of sex for the first time in a long while
Very spooky—on the edge because they can't use all their senses	This spooks deer to their very soul; if you don't know the major travel routes, you won't see many deer
Ignore rain, but feed more during daylight hours	Rely on your scouting patterns and stay in the woods all day; deer could come by any time
Bed near secondary food sources, in very thick stuff; may feed out in the open, however	Hunter pressure is way down; be studious and check out areas that offer both food and cover
Become nocturnal	This is one of those "high-percentage" times; look ahead in weather forecasts for approaching fronts
Will feed heavily within minutes of storm's clearing	Expect deer in more open country than usual
Become confident; may even explore!	Look for parts of deer—ears, legs
Seek refuge, conserve energy; big bucks may feed	Mental aspects the key to success; carry day pack with assortment of aids—soup, blanket, handwarmer, etc.

A good time to search for that heavy-racked buck is after a heavy snowstorm. With the rut behind him and the promise of winter underhoof, an old buck will begin to seriously think of food. That's how this bowhunter bagged this trophy buck.

available a marine band radio that you can tune to a National Weather Service channel for up-to-the-minute forecasts, as well as future trends involving the jet streams.

And as you make note of these forecasts, remember this: Don't be an old fuddy-duddy who's not willing to adjust to the elements.

13

When The Snow Flies

So it finally happened. After patiently waiting, you're going to get your wish. You'd been praying for it along with every skier and snowmobiler in the country, and last night it really snowed. The woods and meadows are covered with a plush carpet of magic crystals!

But how many deer hunters will really benefit from the change in scenery? In spite of its popularity, a fresh snowfall may backfire on far more hunters than it helps.

I know that things haven't always worked out the way I'd dreamed and schemed they would. In spite of my euphoria with a fresh snow, there have been times when a white blanket put a wet blanket on my chances for a particular buck. But nothing I've experienced rivals what once happened to the late Hans Gersbach. How would you like to miss out on a 450-pound, barrel-racked whitetail because of snow? Take heed, and profit from his loss.

Hans was a vanishing breed of deer camp old-timers, a gritty immigrant who hunted for sport, not meat. What a dream-come-true it would have been to kick back over a steamy pot of Russian tea and let the conversation flow with the brew. What unpretentious deer lore to pick up on! But it rarely happened. Hans had a speech impediment, and his English wasn't very good.

But once, just once, one of those precious nuggets of wisdom slipped out between stammering lines.

Picture the halcyon days of logging camps and timber crews. It was a golden era when huge bucks with wrist-thick racks first roamed the big pine country. The particular deer Hans was after had a nickname, as did many legendary bucks, and Hans called him Buster.

"Buster vas not only da biggest deahr I'd ever zeen," Hans reminisced one day, "but his brow tines ver zis tall." With an emphatic gesture, he shoved a pair of stubby hands in front of my face, one at least a foot above the other.

Hans had first found a scrape line skirting an isolated cedar thicket, and it led to the "scrape of scrapes." He said it looked as if a hand grenade had exploded, leaving a patch of ground the size of his living room torn up and shredded to pieces. The immediate area, he said, reeked of buck musk.

Hans knew Buster would return to his calling card once the rut started so he decided to set up an ambush downwind and wait the buck out. It had worked before.

"Right avay I zaw two udder big bucks come to da scrape," Hans told me. "But dey vern't Buster. Dey came for tree dayz in a row, but den it znowed and dat vas dat."

What happened? Hans had to settle for deer track soup. He didn't see another buck, much less a doe, in that area for the rest of the season. Worst of all, the buck he thought he had patterned turned up as a road-kill only a few miles away. It became the talk of the region for many years to come.

"It vas Buster all right," Hans whispered in a quivering voice. "After da znofall, he followed da does dat moved closer to da highvay for food. Vun night he vas hit by a lumber truck. He vas smashed up pretty bad, but somvun scaled him anyvay. Can you accept 450 pounds?"

There are valuable insights to be gleaned from Hans' story.

First, when the first snow flies, a doe's instincts tell her that this is the time to pack on as much weight as possible; soon, winter will settle in and heavy snows are sure to restrict travel and eliminate many food sources. Moreover, she'll need the extra nutrition for her developing young. Her predicament is similar to that of a pregnant woman at a church bazaar. At first, she'll have the luxury of sampling many courses. Eventually, however, some dishes will be depleted, leaving fewer and fewer options. Still, she'll have her own list of "what to shift to next."

Indeed, it would be wise to know these shifts before they

A big non-typical buck like this one taught Ol' Hans a lesson about how snow will change a buck's feeding patterns.

occur. Then, adjusting to new travel patterns as they emerge will keep you in the thick of deer concentrations.

Second, hunters need to know the relationship between snowfall and breeding areas in their specific region. What happens, for instance, to a scrape once it's covered with snow—will a buck re-open it, or will he make a new one? Will does approaching estrus linger in areas where old scrapes are now covered with snow?

Before addressing the first point, let's rehearse some basic facts.

Deer are considered ruminants, or cud-chewing animals. However, recent studies show that when given a choice, they will choose grasses rather than twigs or branches. So, even though they are biologically classified as "browsers," they'd rather be "grazers."

A recent study done on Wisconsin deer confirms this. The stomach contents of 76 road-killed whitetails were examined from April 15 through November 15. The bulk of the food inspected—a full 87 percent—was herbaceous (leafy) material. Another 10 percent of the food volume was made up of fruits and flowers, such as acorns, mushrooms and blackberries. A scant 3 percent was woody twigs and stems. Over 70 different plant types were identified, with aspen leaves being the most important source of food for the deer sampled. Grasses were second.

Conclusion? Deer will switch from soft, leafy plants to harder, woody varieties only when they are forced to do so. Yet, many deer hunters look at "prime deer habitat" with its thick and brushy second-growth vegetation and remark, "Look at all the deer browse." They make a good observation but come to the wrong conclusion.

In the farming belt, the phenomenon of deer switching food sources is easy to keep tabs on. You just have to inventory those cultivated lands that harbor both standing and harvested crops. But don't expect deer to favor unharvested fields over picked ones. The reverse is more often the case. Deer will key in on the residue left behind until supplies have dwindled or snow depths make pawing out today's meal impossible. Then they'll shift over to standing crops.

Which crops? The exact order of preference is a source of much debate. Some veteran hunters and biologists feel that corn is always number one. Other respected authorities insist that deer favor smaller-grained crops whenever accessible. My experiences

Knowing what impact the first snowfall has on feeding habits and the rut will keep you in the thick of deer concentrations. In this chapter the author discusses these effects.

cause me to lean in the direction of the latter camp. The lone exception I often observe is when colder temperatures accompany heavy snowfall and drifting occurs. At that time, corn usually wins out probably because it doubles as wind-breaking cover.

If you think the picture on the deep woods scene is more difficult to draw conclusions from, you're right. That is, if you don't know about slashings that might contain clover and aspen suckers. You probably know that clover is to a deep woods buck what alfalfa is to a farm buck. And you know that once clover beds are layered beneath a blanket of snow, the deer will abandon them overnight.

But did you know that aspen leaves on sucker shoots are extremely hardy? They're capable of resisting many freezing nights before turning colors and falling to the ground. The only trick is to pinpoint the exact locations of aspen logging operations of one, two and three years ago. These clear-cuts will continue to attract feeding does long after other fields have been abandoned for branches and twigs. All you have to do is pattern the entrance and exit routes, as well as identify the bedding sites in thicker cover.

The other consideration raised by Hans' whitetail tale of horrors concerns the relationship between buck sign and snowfall. The key is when the snow falls during a given deer season. An interview with Michigan biologist, John Ozoga, yielded some interesting footnotes.

In spite of all the research scrapes have generated, Ozoga said that biologists still don't know exactly what a scrape is or why it exists. The closest we can get is that they are "some sort of display of dominance" and, perhaps, a source of priming does for the mating ritual. Whether one scrape is "hotter" than another depends mostly upon where it's located. There are isolated scrapes and clusters of scrapes. You'll have to draw your own conclusion, but scrapes should be able to tell whether breeding bucks are still working a particular area. And a breeding buck is one that's more likely to make a mistake than one that's not.

Also, we know that scrape activity peaks just prior to peak breeding activity. After that, it's all downhill. According to Ozoga, an early snowfall will affect scrape activity far differently than one later in the season. And, there are differences worth noting between farm deer and deep woods deer.

"To begin with, you don't normally see a lot of snow when the rut is about to peak," he told me. "But when the two coincide, my bet is that a breeding buck is likely to either stay with a hot doe

Federal research with radio-collared deer indicates that temperature is more of a factor than snow depth in triggering deer movements to traditional wintering yards.

until he breeds her, or continue to act pretty rowdy in his core rutting area. Usually, he won't immediately follow the does as they switch to different food sources. He'll lag behind a bit.''

Snow later on in the season is an entirely different matter, Ozoga said. Bucks will have bred most of the does and a secondary estrus in the North Woods is not likely to occur. Consequently, scrapes are a rare commodity come late November and early December. At this time of year, Ozoga feels that ''scrape areas'' are not nearly as significant as they might have been in late October or early November. But there is a minor exception.

''In the lower Midwest agricultural areas,'' he said, '' you will see a sudden upsurge in breeding activity in mid-December. That's when many fawn does will go into heat for the first time. Scrapes become significant again, and they should be taken into account regardless of the snow conditions.''

Now when you add Ozoga's thoughts to Hans' tale of horrors, you might come up with more questions than answers. For instance, why did the other two bucks show up and not Buster? And, why not a single doe?

The answers will come once we discuss the final clue to locating deer in snowy conditions: the yarding instinct.

Federal researcher L. David Mech has radio-tracked deer

while investigating the many mysteries of yarding migrations. Some of his findings can affect deer hunting strategy.

For example:

Temperature is more of a factor than snow depth in triggering deer movements toward traditional yards.

Moderating temperatures were observed to have influenced deer in a reverse role: rising temperatures drew deer out of their winter yards and back toward summer ranges.

In some areas, the deer made a beeline for time-honored yards, traveling distances of 20 to 30 miles within a day or two.

In other areas, more gradual migrations toward the densest cover of the non-winter range were observed, especially following significant snowfalls.

The hunter who is greeted with an early winter during the deer season, or the one who opts for late-season slug, bow or blackpowder hunting, needs to familiarize himself with how deer yard up in northern climes. He is particularly vulnerable to becoming "trapped" between deer movements, unless he correctly analyzes the unfolding conditions before him.

First ask your state fish and game department questions about one particular hunting area: Where do deer yard up? Do the deer make a swift move toward a yard, or do they gradually move to heavier cover? In northeastern Minnesota, for example, radical, long-distance movements are more common than in Michigan, where Ozoga reports a gradual shift toward heavy cover that "might not be ideal shelter, but offers better browse than the core of a yard."

Second, make note of the thickest cover in your hunting area. If you think you're already hunting the thick stuff, look again. Chances are, you've been compromising and choosing areas with small openings or those with scattered "shooting lanes." They just won't do this time of the year. The deer move into the kind of thickets that you almost have to walk backwards to get through. Those at the headwaters of a waterway, or river are always a good place to start your search. So are cedar swamps abutting hardwood ridges, pine plantations and hemlock stands.

Knowing where to hunt deer when the snow flies is helpful only if you know how to hunt them during this special time. There is really only one way: harder. Ironically, many hunters relax a bit and think it's easier now than without snow. Sure, the deer stand out more in the snow, but don't forget that you, too, stand out more readily to the deer. Also deer will turn to their eyes to help

Research shows that scrape activity peaks just prior to peak breeding activity. However, an early snowfall will affect scrape activity far differently than one later in the season.

confirm their noses' suspicions, because the snow will muffle every sound.

You should follow suit. Instead of relaxing your eyes when the snow flies, work them overtime in hopes of seeing deer well before they see you. You'll rarely get a double-take from a big buck and this is one time of the year they'll spook at the slightest movement, regardless of wind direction. What a sinking feeling it is to find a fresh set of big tracks with 20-foot spaces between them.

This leaves only one option—don a pair of binoculars whenever it snows. To get the most out of your optics, slow down and check out anything that looks "different." I've found that a deer's nose sticks out best, followed by its eyes, ears and white chest.

Without binoculars, it's next to almost impossible to tell a big deer from an average one in dense cover. Once, I spotted what appeared to be a nice buck and was about to launch a 180-grain bullet from my .308 when I thought I'd take a closer peek with the glasses. The wind was right and I was well hidden, so why not? It turned out to be an overstuffed forkhorn, and I decided to let it go, which turned out to be a good idea. A decent 10-pointer showed up only moments later. That's one lesson I'll never forget.

Another trick for spotting deer before they spot you is to use your peripheral vision for picking up movement, rather than relying strictly upon head-on eyesight. There is a trick to it: avoid staring at the suspected target. Instead, look off to one side and let your peripheral vision tell you if there's something alive there. I'm continually amazed at how this part of the human anatomy functions, and it can be a great asset to a deer hunter.

Deer hunting and fresh snow seem to be made for each other. But it can be a love/hate relationship if the snow pays a visit during the deer season and you're caught out of position. Remember, there's a big difference between responding to changing circumstances and reacting in a panic when the changes come.

14

Deer Tracks:
There Is A Difference

Different weather types determine different hunting tactics; that, we've seen. But one type of precipitation, in particular, opens up a whole new world to a special breed of big buck hunters—the tracker. And you can bet that when the snow flies, this individual will be out practicing his art on the trail of the whitetail buck.

But tracking is more than an art to some. For trophy hunters such as Noble Carlson, tracking a big buck is more of a science. As a matter of fact, it was Carlson who told me flat-out that I was "spreading myths" when I once penned a statement that there is no single, reliable method to tell a buck's track from a large doe's. I was up to my ears in a good argument.

"All you've got are theories," he said. "I've got the facts. I spend almost as much time in the woods as the deer during the fall, except I don't sleep out there."

The fact that he's killed lots of big bucks is more than incidental trivia. But just shooting a lot of deer didn't give instant credibility to Noble's argument. It was *how* he did it that bent my ears: *he tracked them.*

"Every buck track shares certain characteristics," he continued, "that clearly distinguishes it from a doe's. I'll show you."

Although I had lots of company in the argument, (I had never read anything on the subject to the contrary), I was curious to see

The top view of deer hooves show you how a buck's hoof (right) is worn and rounded. The hoof on the left, menwhile, belongs to a younger doe. You'll see the difference also in the tracks, as shown on the following pages.

what he could "show" me, so the next chance we got we were bending over fresh deer tracks behind his house.

"Look at this track," he said pointing to a large print in the snow. "It's definitely a big buck. What first strikes you is how the hoofprint arcs out from the tip like an upside-down Valentine's heart.

"A doe's print, like this one here," he explained pointing, "is much different. Instead of a blunt tip and a broad, wide arc, her hooves don't curve much before they angle down to the bottom of the pad."

I wasn't quite with it, so he stooped down and drew a pair of tracks accentuating what he had just explained to me. "See now what I mean?"

"I think so, but I'm not totally convinced every deer shares those characteristics," I said.

"Well, let's go to another section and try it on another set of tracks," he said.

So we did. This time he asked me to identify them. According

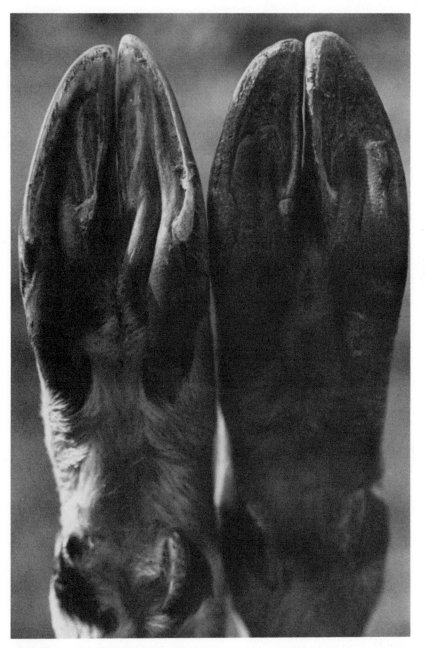

The bottom view of deer hooves also shows you how an older deer's hooves (right) are worn, rounded and less defined.

to his criteria, I hit a bull's-eye on the first three. But then he set me up.

"What's this one?" he asked.

"I think it's a buck," I said. "It's pretty big to be a doe."

"Nope," he said. "You let the size of the track fool you. That has little to do with it. Even little bucks' tracks arc out from the tip like I showed you. This one's a doe. I've seen her in this area for a few years and she sure is big for a doe."

I looked at the tracks again. Either I was beginning to lose my mind or he had something here. It all seemed very convincing.

Since then I've analyzed just about every track I've seen; I guess it's time to eat a little humble pie—Noble was right, I was wrong.

I challenge you to prove us wrong. Next time you find a sharp deer track—whether it is in earth or snow—pay strict attention to its overall shape. If your first impression is that the spoor drops down from the tip in a gentle but almost immediate slope, and the pads appear to be fairly close together, it's a doe's track.

Conversely, if you think the print is rather wide, angling out immediately at the tip, with some space between the pads, you're looking at a buck's spoor.

It's also easy to tell an older buck from a young one, according to Noble.

"The older a buck gets, the more rounded the tips of the tracks become. They just plain wear down from constant contact with rocks, logs and other obstructions," he said.

Are there any clues to the size of a buck, from the tracks he leaves behind? This takes more experience with tracking deer, but Noble's answer is a definite "yes." Heavier bucks always leave a deeper track, he says, but you have to be careful not to be fooled by tracks over soft surfaces—creekbeds, moist gravel or organic material. Moreover, the dew claws should appear in snow two inches or deeper, or you could be looking at an adolescent animal as opposed to a full-bodied mature specimen.

It's great to know that buck tracks are wider, more blunt at the tip, and doe tracks are thinner and more elongated...but what if you don't have very fresh tracks to work with? The more a track ages, the less sharp its definition becomes. It can be confusing, as gravity, oxidation and evaporation work their effects upon the prints.

Fortunately, there are more clues. For starters, bucks usually drag their feet when travelling at an undisturbed, casual pace.

Notice how the track on the left is wider, more rounded and less precise? More than likely this is an older deer's print. The track on the right, meanwhile, is narrow and more clearly defined. This print probably belongs to a young deer.

Does, on the other hand, pick up their feet and almost prance atop the ground.

So bucks saunter while does do the high-step. Also, there are differences in the trails they leave behind. For example, the routes taken offer several hints to the sex of the animal. Bucks, especially those with large racks, tend to go over and around obstructions such as fallen logs and isolated thickets. Does are likely to do the opposite, crawling under the obstructions and weaving *through* the thickets.

Their line of travel is generally different and can often be conclusively ascertained. If the tracks you're trailing tend to take short, direct routes from one geographic area to another, they likely belong to a buck—especially if they are solitary tracks cutting through the woods. Does seem to meander—almost aimlessly at times—as they work a given area. And they travel in groups much more often than bucks.

If there is snow on the ground, pay close attention to urine deposits along the trail—they could tip off the sex of their maker. Again, there is a distinguishable difference between the two; the result of a doe's urination is a larger splotch on the snow, with an irregular pattern, whereas a buck's is a more precise perforation of the snow. And if you spot an orange or reddish-stained urine, you could have a doe in heat in the vicinity—almost as good as the buck himself.

Another trick is to carefully study the tracks surrounding a scrape. Because both bucks and does traffic the surrounding and immediate area, you can't afford to be sloppy, nor can you take it for granted that all tracks leading directly from the scrape are a buck's. You'll just have to look for more clues, keeping the above pointers in mind, and continue tracking the set that looks the most promising. The key is to take it slow and not yield to the temptation of trying to catch up when the trails come together and then break apart again. I nearly shot my first bedded buck by following that advice recently. Here's what happened:

I had carefully approached my stand across a starlit landscape about an hour before sunrise one cold morning, and just what I was trying to prevent occurred—a group of deer spooked ahead of me on the trail leading to my tree stand. My hunch said they were does because they whistled and snorted at me about a dozen times as they vanished into the hollow darkness. I have found that bucks, when unexpectedly startled like that, will either whistle once or at

Here's Noble with two bucks that he and his hunting partner tracked down and outsmarted. His tips in this chapter are backed by his proven track record.

most twice before they're gone, or they'll remain silent, leaving no such signal to nearby deer.

By 1:00 p.m. I was shivering uncontrollably on my stand so I made a circle around the area that brought me back to the point where I had jumped the does earlier. In the process I found a lone set of tracks that were definitely a good buck's. Sure as shootin', when he got to where he intercepted those does, he made a straight line for their bedding area. It was amusing to note how he cut right through all their circuitous meandering and ended up on their trail again a few hundred yards ahead.

But that's when things got very confusing. Apparently he bred one or more does—there were tracks upon tracks with some skid marks, with the trail eventually fanning out in several directions. Unfortunately, a stiff wind had whipped up, filling the prints with a light dusting of snow, so I could no longer make out any differences from the two largest sets. It was getting late, but I knew if I could untangle that puzzle, I might be able to sneak up on the bedding buck—at least silent travel was possible with the wind and soft snow helping me out, so I gave it a shot.

By taking it a step at a time, I unraveled the right set out of the maze; there were curled wood shavings on top of the snow next to the trail—a fresh rub! As I continued on into a quartering wind, I could sense a golden opportunity. Soon I could barely see a dark form underneath a clump of balsams, and I prepared myself for a quick shot.

About the *only* thing that could go wrong, at this point, however, did. My attention was so intense on the trail ahead that I failed to notice a doe a mere 20 yards off to the side. At my next step she let loose with a series of whistles as she bounced out of sight, alarming the buck and startling the wits out of me. He was a fine animal, although no trophy by Boone & Crockett standards. Yet it would have been a real trophy experience to have tracked him down and then taken him. Oh well....

So the next time you hear or read that a buck's track can't be distinguished from a doe's, don't believe it. And don't be afraid to admit it if you used to think so. Humble pie tastes real good with venison stew—but you might have to eat the pie before you can get to the stew.

15

You Can Track A Buck

One tracker who rarely finds himself eating humble pie is trophy hunter Noble Carlson. Carlson, as we've discussed earlier, is a real expert when it comes to following the track of a big buck. I consider it an honor to have hunted with this whitetail enthusiast, especially as a student of his expertise, even though I didn't think it was that big of a deal at the time.

The two of us were fast onto a big buck's track, and the drama should have been mounting like the last page of a best selling suspense novel.

But it wasn't—at least for me.

To be perfectly honest, I was pretty darn nonchalant about tracking down a buck. I mean, who really depends on this method to get a deer? Sure, it's nice to follow fresh tracks in the woods after a new snowfall, see what the deer have been doing and snoop around where they used to be. But by the time you get close enough for a glimpse, much less a decent shot, they'll be long gone, I thought. Big bucks, as the overworked cliche goes, don't get that way by being dumb. Right?

"Shh!"

Carlson was stopped dead in his tracks, and his warning meant that it was a good time to be quiet and alert. His blue Scandinavian eyes glowered beneath bristling, bleached-orange eyebrows.

"Murray, how am I ever going to make a tracker out of you?"

I did not respond. What could I say? Moments earlier, we had been half-trotting right on top of a deer trail. Why, Noble himself had snapped three twigs. I heard them easily (and I was counting). Now he was yapping at me to be totally silent. Tracking deer, Noble Carlson style, was weird.

Wait a minute—what was I thinking?! This was no silly safari I was on with some crazy bush pilot guide. This was Noble Carlson, a man who had already shot four bucks that fall—(it's legal to group hunt in Minnesota) all by tracking—and well over 100 from seasons past. This was a guy who never made outlandish-sounding statements about anything in the outdoors, unless he could back it up.

Still, the gnawing feeling that it could only happen to him when I wasn't around tugged at me. After all, I was just two steps behind him.

"That buzzard," he said. "I'm starting to get mad."

"What...why?"

He flicked the barrel of his Model 722 Remington through the snow in disgust. Next to the little depression he made was a fresh deer bed. We'd just spooked it out ahead of us. Just how I thought it would go.

"He must have heard me shush you, Murray. How am I going to make a tracker out of you?"

Under normal circumstances, Noble would leave the buck alone and try to cut another fresh buck track. From nearly 30 years of tracking whitetails, he has learned that it is usually futile to try to stay on top of a spooked buck—they'll just outrun you. But this time was a little different. Instead, he knelt down and sized up the bed. As he looked north, he asked me how bad I wanted the buck.

As a devout stand hunter, I'd seen many a day when the deer weren't moving. If I could track bucks on those days, I could be a lot more effective...

"Look," he said, reading my mind, "I know you aren't even sure if this was a buck or a doe. But I know. Get a sniff of this."

He tossed me a chunk of snow, stained yellow from the hock gland where the buck had laid. It was rancid. It was musky, all male. I was convinced.

"He's a trophy buck...by your standards," he teased, referring to a comment I had made earlier; I had said that any deer with 10 points and thick beams would make "my" record book. "Look at the width of the track. See how deep it penetrates the snow? And

If anyone can track a big buck and get close enough for a shot, it is Noble Carlson. He has more than 30 years of practice and consistent success.

the tips are rounded off pretty good. No young buck has round tips like these.

"If you wanna go for it, I can guarantee at least a 50-50 shot at him, but you gotta do exactly what I say."

Guarantee? Gads, here he goes again, I thought.

"Whatever you say, Nobel."

Last night, on his kitchen table, he had scratched out his basic strategy over the back of a Snicker's candy wrapper. He told me how important it was to "read" the tracks and make the correct interpretation of what the buck was doing. It sounded so simple. When the buck ran, we were going to run. When it slowed down, we were to do the same. Finally, when the buck left signs that it was about to bed down, or better yet, was feeding between bedding stints, we would sneak up on it from an unsuspecting angle.

I remember the anxiety I had about the prospects of having to make a good shot at a running animal, something with which I hadn't had a great deal of experience or success. But Noble said it shouldn't worry me.

"Of all the bucks I've tracked down," he told me, "I'd bet over 90 percent never saw me or knew what hit them."

Another fear I had was the one that must plague all hunters who give tracking even a feeble try: How do you know if the deer is a mile away or just over the next hill? Again, Noble had a reassuring explanation with plenty of experience upon which to draw.

"You can boil it all down to two things," he began. "First, when that buck is on a runway, he's moving, looking for company—you know, a hot doe. Otherwise he'd be off on his own, looking for a safe place to feed or bed down. So when he's on a trail, you gotta work to keep up with him. And you can't keep up if you're worrying about being quiet. Besides, it doesn't matter a lick, because he's going to be way up ahead, and would probably associate any noise on the trail, at this point, with that of another deer.

"And second, when his tracks start meandering, splitting off to the side here, straying over there, you know he's slowed way down. When you get to tracks like these, you can't make a sound and you can't be on the trail, either. If you are, you're dead, because he'll be spending more time watching his back-trail than watching where he's going."

Suddenly, this all began to click for me. We had jogged across the runway and slowed down when we saw the buck's track

When tracking a buck, Noble Carlson says that you should keep up with the buck.
When he moves at a quick trot, you do the same. When he slows, you slow.

splinter off the main trail. We were just about to pull the final maneuver of getting off the tracks when we spooked the buck up ahead. Many hunters are proficient at getting on a fresh track, but the reason most of us fail, from Noble's point of view, is that we don't know how to handle what he calls the "end-around."

"When I told you I'd teach you how to track up a buck, you probably had it in your head that we were going to sneak up on a deer in its track. That's how everyone thinks it's done. But I hardly ever walk up to a buck from his trail—they're too busy watching it for timber wolves and guys like you. No way.

"The trick is to dodge around and up ahead when you see him monkeying around, feeding or looking for a place to bed down. While he's watching his backtrail you'll be sneaking in from the side at an angle he won't be watching. But you've got to be quiet and see him first."

From its bed, the buck had literally jumped the span of a mid-sized river—I marked it off at 20 paces between the prints in the snow. The bucks Noble hunts are some the biggest in North America, averaging 225 to 240 pounds, field-dressed. Northern Minnesota deer have to be big and tough or they won't survive the harsh winters and the relentless pursuit of wolf packs on their backs year-round.

We stayed on the trail for 100 yards before the tracks started to tighten up again.

"See here. This is a good sign. Notice how he is already starting to slow down at a more normal pace? He couldn't have winded us."

That much I could understand. Countless were the times when a deer I had jumped continued on with those loping Olympic strides. Those are the ones to leave behind. But not this one. And he seemed intent on going in one direction, slicing northeast across a northwest wind.

If he had decided to circle around to wind us, we would have given up on this guy, too. No sense trailing an edgy buck when there are plenty of others much more vulnerable to Noble's system, even along the edge of this wilderness area, where the head count is often less than five deer to the square mile.

The buck carved a trail along a creek bed, pretty much in a straight line, no meandering, no feeding or bedding yet. Then we found a fresh rub at the edge of a clearing, where thin wood shavings powdered the base of a five-inch cedar. A rush of adrenaline pumped through me—only a heavy buck would take on a tree that thick.

It was time for another major lesson in tracking. After the buck had made that rub, he had waltzed right down the middle of the clearing, not along the edges like one might expect a smart animal to do. It was time to make a decision. The right one would allow us to continue the game, a wrong one would end it right there.

"What are we going to do now?" Noble asked. He was setting me up.

"Well, we gotta keep up don't we? The buck isn't showing any signs of letting up or anything."

"Not necessarily. This is one of their tricks that most guys blow it on." Then he bent down and drew a diagram in the snow, showing how bucks like to pause on the opposite end of an opening, so they can watch their backtrack. "They do it all the time, especially when they're headed into the wind."

"So what do we do?" I asked.

"Every time a buck pulls this on you, there's only one thing to do: Circle around the opening. Sometimes he'll be there, sometimes he'll continue on. Let's go see."

It took, what seemed to me, an awful long time to skirt the edge. And, sure enough, the buck was nowhere to be found. But Noble was dead on. Tracks left behind told the story of a buck pausing in two places on the inside edge of the opening. I could easily imagine him looking over his shoulder, waiting for some dummy to walk through the clearing. Then he'd snort the wits out of his pursuer and dash off.

The trail continued on in a relatively straight path, coursing through open aspens and balsam thickets. Each time, we circled around the open stuff and snuck through the thickets. It was rough country with no roads, and I shuddered to think that Noble never carries a compass. He has an uncanny sense of direction in the woods and, he says, he has never been lost. But he would never recommend that anyone go without a compass. Still, he got a kick out of my insistence on carrying two compasses.

Now the trail was joined by another set and within 50 yards there were three different sets to unravel—another one of my fears when attempting to track down a specific animal. This was a time for utmost caution, requiring attention to every detail. Confusion could easily set in if the tracker didn't keep sight of "the big picture," looking ahead to where the tracks were going. Of course, this was second nature to Noble, because he surveyed the country

When a set of tracks you are following is joined by other tracks, keep in mind the "big picture" by looking ahead to where your buck's tracks might be going.

ahead more than he doted over the tracks anyway.

By examining each set it was evident that a fawn and a doe had become part of the drama and an interesting footnote emerged for another valuable lesson in tracking.

"Ah, the plot thickens," Noble whispered while bending over some droppings, squishing one between his fingers. "They're still soft. And that little one is a fawn buck. He'll show us what's going on."

It made no sense at the moment, but soon did. Over the next quarter-mile, the three traveled together with the smallest track occasionally darting off to one side. Each time it happened, Noble

When a buck's tracks start to meander, get off his trail and circle around and ahead of him so you can take a shot like this hunter is about to make while the buck is preoccupied watching his backtrail.

pointed it out as if it was something significant that I should know. Finally, I had to ask what it meant.

"The buck is chasing him off," he whispered. "But the fawn buck keeps coming back to the doe. That tells me that the buck wants to jump the doe but she isn't quite ready yet. The next time we circle around we could get right on top of the buck. He's distracted, but we can't forget about the other two."

Our next end-around taught me another lesson. The fawn and the doe had disappeared from the scene and the buck had started circling back toward our direction. Quickly, Noble changed his course with me on his heels. We made a wide arc in the opposite direction of the buck's circle. Without any warning, the buck attempted to check his back trail, and he almost caught us off guard. We were able to cover a lot of ground in a hurry without tipping him off. It's another "buck trick" Noble had learned from years of tracking.

Noble wears felt liners inside zippered rubber overshoes so he can feel the landscape underfoot, avoid setting his weight in the wrong places and nimbly roll forward as he walks. He made me promise to likewise equip my feet, or he would refuse to enter the woods with me. "Otherwise, we'd just be wasting our time," he said.

We picked up the track again at the edge of a small meadow. We had crossed some older tracks on the way that would have sidetracked me if I was on my own. Fortunately, Noble has not only learned how to differentiate a buck's track from a doe's, but also how to distinguish one buck's track from another. At first, to me, they all looked alike. Sure there were big, medium and small ones. But soon I was sure his method of looking at the tips, the width and the arch of the spoor was indeed foolproof. But graduating to the point of telling individual bucks apart was a big step. The only confidence I had that we might be on the same buck came from Noble's confidence. He took the time to reassure me.

"Your buck here, isn't real old, but he's got pretty old, rounded hooves. Maybe a five- or a six-year-old. Those others were only about three or four years old. They looked big, but their tips were much sharper and pointed. Besides, yours is missing a small chip out of his left front hoof. I'm surprised you haven't noticed it. How am I going to make a tracker out of you?"

By now it was snowing, with leaden skies to the west promising little relief. The tracks were beginning to fill in almost as fast as they were being made. This was a time for perfect

Here is another "buck trick" that Noble Carlson has learned. This big buck is pausing on the opposite end of an opening to check his backtrail.

tracking—under almost impossible conditions. It would be perfect for the tracker who had cut a fresh track and could stay on it, because he could silently move in for the kill.

But it can be impossible at times when your track gets intermingled with others; a two-day-old track and a brand new one will both fill up and look identical. When this happens, all you can do is wait for an hour or so, and look for tracks again. The ones you'll be able to see will obviously be fresh, because all the others will be covered up.

Noble's all-time favorite situation to track down a big buck is during the season's first or second snowfall. He can "just about ride their backs" under these conditions. He's got four solid reasons. First, the deer haven't been pushed by wolves for seven or eight months. Second, they haven't been pushed by trackers for 10 months. Third, big bucks won't go very far once it starts snowing heavily, so Noble doesn't have to cover much ground. And fourth, the deer think they still blend in with their surroundings, and they are apt to stand around in fairly open patches.

"If a guy isn't tracking then," he says, "he's missing the closest thing he'll ever get to a sure bet on a buck."

Luckily, we didn't run across any other tracks that afternoon. But the snow was getting so deep it was hard to tell which way the buck was heading. At one point, he headed over a hill and veered around a beaver pond, making a little loop. Which way was he going? In a muffled voice with his chopper mitten over his lips, Noble explained an easy way to tell:

"I'll show you a little trick, Murray. See these little tufts of snow? They're kicked up by the buck's paws after he lifts them up and out of the snow. In deep snow, they always point in the direction the buck is heading, because they are pushed out in front of the track."

When we reached a small stream, I noticed how the skim ice was broken by the buck's fresh track, though the rest of the stream remained frozen over. I pointed proudly to my observant discovery and, immediately, Noble wrenched my head with his left hand, his eyes glowering again. A growl grew in his throat. But it was too late.

The fresh bed, 60 yards away, meant only one thing: We had spooked the buck again. Ordinarily, the buck will give you a warning that he is about to bed down. He'll skip from one balsam or cedar or spruce to another, turning around while scenting and gazing over his backtrack. This time he hadn't.

Noble helps Jeff Murray drag out his trophy buck, which the author took during his
first tracking lesson.

"Damn, I saw it coming," Noble said in disgust. "When it snows heavy like this, sometimes they just go to a bed right away. He must've seen your movement."

The sun was less than an hour from setting, so it was too late to look for another track. From tracking in this area for many years, Noble knew where the buck might be headed—a knoll at the tip of a large tag alder swamp. It was the perfect place for a buck under hot pursuit to hide out, because any predator would announce its presence when it broke through the swamp, and the buck could lay near the edge, winding the other side. If we could get there first...

We took the side of the swamp opposite the buck, and were

squeezing around the outer edge when it happened. Like magic, we picked up the buck's trail, and I thought I saw where another deer had joined in from the west. Instead of continuing ahead or making a circle, Noble whirled around to the west with his gun up.

"Are you going to take him, or do I have to shoot your deer for you?"

I looked to the west and saw the buck standing with its nose up and ears back. He was looking over the trail he had just made. I don't remember pulling the trigger, much less taking aim. But somehow the gun went off. And the deer bolted.

"You hit him!" Noble yelled.

The buck didn't go very far, less than 200 yards. The bullet had grazed his heart and punctured both lungs. His massive neck was swollen with rut, and the base of his rack was as thick as my wrist, 10 points strong. Noble flipped him over and brushed the snow off of his front hooves.

"Here's your buck, all right," he said with a bit of pride. "See the chip in the hoof?"

I glowed. But how had he done it? How had he known to look over to the west, where that track appeared to join in?

"That was just another trick," he said. "He doubled back down his track and stood off to the side of the trail. He was expecting us to be trailing behind."

It was one more "buck trick" that's worth remembering.

16

Backtrack Your Buck

But the Noble Carlsons of the world are not always around to help you sort out the mysteries surrounding the tracks of big whitetail bucks. Sometimes, while tracking the elusive white-tailed deer and testing your ability to distinguish between buck and doe tracks, a "hopeless" situation can become the spark for a brilliant discovery. Like a meteor out of the dark, something hits you, leaving a lasting impression on how you view things.

The discovery of this sort that tops my list occurred several seasons ago. Nothing else I've ever learned about hunting whitetails has proven as helpful in bagging bucks. It started with an unexpected snow squall one November afternoon.

Snowflakes were falling like goose feathers, almost touching one another, and I could see no farther than the tip of my nocked arrow. Snow worked its way from my hunched shoulders onto my neck. Four well-worn trails—two on each side of my tree—formed a near, tic-tac-toe grid. Even though I had spent three fruitless days there, I was confident that I would eventually get a deer.

Now for the hopeless situation: I was shivering uncontrollably, my teeth chattering like castanets. It seemed to be snowing sideways as I slid down the old aspen tree.

I hadn't gone 100 yards, quartering into the wind, when I jumped a big deer that romped into a tag alder thicket. I didn't notice whether or not it had a rack.

Halfheartedly, I circled the alders in hopes of intercepting the deer on the other side. I easily picked up the tracks in the fresh snow and followed them until they doubled back into the thicket. For some reason, I decided to follow them back to see where the deer had come from, instead of where it might be going. This led to my discovery.

First, I found a large bed, then another. When I found a line of fresh scrapes, the full impact of what I was onto finally hit me. Here, in 20 minutes of scouting, I had located a buck's hangout! These were fresh beds and scrapes, being used during the day, during the hunting season! I wasted no time putting my portable tree stand between the beds and scrapes. Then I got out of there.

Like clockwork, the thick-necked eight-pointer sauntered by my stand the very next day. When he turned broadside, 12 yards away, I drove my broadhead into his heart. The buck dropped at the edge of the alder thicket, not more than 50 yards away. So my discovery paid off. What's even more intriguing is how that spot has continued to yield a buck each year since. Even though it doesn't look nearly as promising as the stand near the tic-tac-toe deer trails, that's where the bucks always seem to be during the hunting season. And it was no fluke. Other hunters have used my "backtracking" method to achieve similar results.

Backtracking is not a replacement for pre-season scouting, nor is it a shortcut to a freezer full of venison. It does, however, answer the questions that most field reconnaissance trips only begin to raise: Which scrapes are active and which ones are dormant? Which ones are worked during the day? Which trails are used during the day? In the morning? In the afternoon? Where do bucks bed during the day? Where do they feed?

Indeed, backtracking is much like target-sighting a scoped rifle after it has been bore-sighted. It works especially well for the deep-woods deer hunter who is often beset with the difficult task of untangling whitetail patterns where there is no discernible difference between bedding and feeding areas. Where I hunt, deer feed, bed and breed all in the same cover. It does me little good just to find bedding and feeding areas. I need to pinpoint a buck's daytime whereabouts. Backtracking is the key.

Some hunters certainly will ask, "Why give up a day or two of hunting, especially during the rut?" I have three, short answers to that question. One, you could bump into another buck traveling through the territory. (I once filled my tag this way by shooting a fat forkhorn on the last day of the season.) Two, you could run into

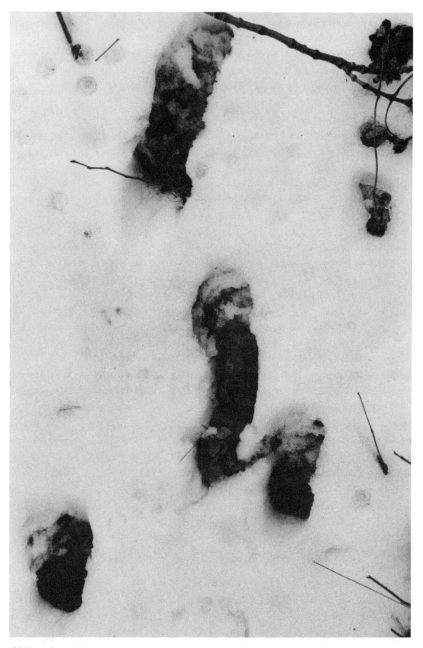

Old tracks in the snow like these are discernible by the icy crystalization around the hoofprint. A fresh track will be more crisp. Successful trackers learn by practice and listening to experienced hunters.

By intercepting a track and following it backwards, you'll be able to locate the deer's bedding area. A big buck's bedroom will usually have scrapes and a number of rubs in a concentrated area.

the buck you're backtracking as he completes his circuit. (This happened to me once and I was as surprised as the buck.) And three, you'll be in the woods during the rut, and, whenever you're in the woods during the rut, almost anything can happen.

Backtracking often turns out to be a learning experience from the ground up because most hunters rarely track deer nowadays, and those who do are usually banking on finding where a deer is going, not where it has been.

The first order of business is finding a buck's fresh track. The easiest of all to track and age is a fresh set of prints in three to four inches of snow. A brand-new track is letter-perfect, with a crisp, sharp outline, noticeable even between each hoof mark. As time passes, the edges become less distinct; the track will acquire a feathered look; and ice particles will begin to fall into the depression. Despite these rudimentary rules of thumb, I used to have great difficulty in determining how fresh a track really was.

The same basic drive that motivates a buck like this to paw out a scrape will drive him to return and check it regularly during the rut. You can backtrack to a line of scrapes and position your stand where you will have the best shot.

Just when I'd decide, someone would disagree, causing me to second-guess myself. Not any more. Now, I can spot a truly fresh track nine out of 10 times. You can, too.

All you have to do is get hold of a deer's leg, with hoof attached, of course. Ask your hunting buddies, a butcher or a local conservation officer (be sure to tell him what you're up to). Wait for snow. Then depress the hoof with about 40 or 50 pounds of pressure (check on the bathroom scale to see how this ''feels'') in the snow. Observe. Do it again, and again, and again. Soon, you can have a friend make a number of tracks to test you on finding the freshest ones.

Aging a track is nearly as important as determining the sex of its maker. You could end up wasting a lot of energy if you follow tracks made at the wrong time of day. Here's what happened to a friend of mine.

Gary had just completed his tracking, certain he was set up over some hot scrapes. He had determined that the buck would enter his scrapes from the south when that was the downwind position; otherwise, the buck would enter these particular scrapes from the west, where a large spruce bog buttressed the knoll his calling cards were laid out on. For three days, Gary saw nothing but blue jays and squirrels. One night, after dinner in camp, he decided to switch areas, so he took a flashlight and went back to retrieve his portable stand. A huge 10-pointer bolted from underneath the treestand when Gary was no more than an arm's length away.

Back at camp, we analyzed the situation. Why was the buck using the scrapes at night and not during the day? It appeared that we were back to square one.

"Are you sure it wasn't a different buck from the one you were tracking?" I asked.

"Can't be," he said. "Those tracks are a perfect match."

"Are you sure they were fresh tracks?" I asked. "Maybe they were from the night before."

"Yeah, they were fresh, all right." he said. "I cut the tracks first thing in the morning, right after the snow ended..."

We looked at each other in astonishment as the revelation hit us simultaneously.

Gary, indeed, had been backtracking a buck's fresh tracks. But the more he tracked them, the farther into the previous night they took him. He recalled that it had taken at least two miles of tracking for him to find the scrapes. We had simply forgotten to think backwards. From this lesson, we know that the only track to backtrack, if you want to know what a buck is doing during the day, is one made in the afternoon or toward dusk.

If there is a trick to aging a track, it starts with understanding gravity. After a deer's hoofprint disturbs objects from their natural position, the tracks will look "fresh" to the discerning eye only until the disturbed objects settle. How long does this take? On bare earth, about five hours. In the snow, 10 minutes to an hour. If you get on all fours and scrutinize tracks with a small flashlight, you will be amazed at how simple and constant this principle is.

Unfortunately, many hunters become intimidated by the notion of tracking a deer without snow. However, anyone with enough

This bowhunter backtracked a buck he jumped and found a series of scrapes like this one.

patience to sit on a deer stand for a day can learn to do it.

Most of us have seen deer tracks along river bottoms and creekbeds. Whitetails are bottomland creatures. The simplest procedure upon finding such a trail is to smooth out all the tracks at midmorning, then come back during the afternoon and observe. If there are fresh tracks coming directly from high ground, where big bucks are most apt to make their scrapes, try backtracking. If you find any beds along the way, that may be a good area for a stand.

In just a few seasons of backtracking, I've learned more about deer behavior than I ever thought possible. A day spent backtracking is worth at least five seasons in the woods.

A topographic map is an invaluable asset in plotting your strategy. But even the best maps available are far too minuscule for me, so I like to have the particular map section I'm interested in enlarged to the size of a full notebook-size page. Then, I mark deer signs as well as travel routes, benchmarks and helpful hints to keep things in perspective. An aerial photo, enlarged to the same scale, is also helpful.

If you've been coming up short after doing all that you can to find big bucks in your area, try backtracking. You won't be disappointed.

17

Know Your
Buck's Weight

A nd finally, no book on trophy deer would be complete without a chapter on how you can tell how big that buck really is. No aspect of deer hunting has been debated as much as this, and it's surprising how many hunters know so little when it comes down to the weight of the problem. Never was this more evident than in a conversation I heard a few seasons back.

It was one of those still, cloudy nights—the kind that carries voices like a telephone wire. I remember it all so well because it was their chatter that helped me get from my deer stand to the road that November evening. I had lost both of my compasses and couldn't see a thing in the dark.

Their conversation was a common one, no doubt carried on over many a plate of deer-shack stew. It seems one of them had nailed a decent buck, and while they were dragging it out they ended up arguing over how much it weighed.

"This monster's gotta go at least 220," I overheard one of them say triumphantly.

"Wanna bet?" replied the other. "More like 250!"

When I came upon them, we exchanged pleasantries with the usual congratulatory fanfare that accompanies the taking of a thick-necked, 10-point buck. Although most conversations die shortly after they begin, this one grew and grew. Somehow, I found myself the appointed arbitrator of the dispute. But rather than merely guess the buck's weight, I simply did what any well-equipped deer hunter would do: I pulled from my pack a little gizmo tailor-made for the situation.

"I declare this buck to be about...190 pounds, give or take five pounds."

"One-ninety?!" they shrieked in unison.

Before we separated, I handed my business card to the teenager who shot the buck. "If you get it weighed on a good scale," I said, "give me a call and let me know what you find out."

"Sure, be glad to," he said.

A full year went by before I got the call. A shy voice explained that it was "the guy with the deer." I'd seen lots of guys with deer that year, could he refresh my memory?

"Well," he began sheepishly, "my deer ended up having a little weight problem."

Turns out his buck didn't weigh 250 pounds, or 220 pounds...or even 200 pounds. It weighed 192 pounds.

How is it that my "guess" was so close? Well, I used a little formula. You see, a number of researchers, colleges and institutes throughout the country have been studying whitetail body conformities. And in the process, a lot of research has lead to several formulas for determining a deer's body weight. All are based on the time-honored method of estimating cattle weight by taking a heart girth measurement.

Which one is the most accurate? Now that's a darn good question. Unfortunately, there isn't a simple answer. To make matters worse, there are a variety of "deer tapes" sold commercially that only add to the confusion. These tape measures can help you calculate everything from a deer's dressed weight to how much meat you should get back from the butcher. Some are fairly accurate for a specific locale, but most are not. Why? In the words of Bob Giles, professor of wildlife management in Virginia, "There are big local differences, and everyone ought to develop an equation for their area." The reason for all the differences is the lack of similarity of body conformity among whitetails.

Part of the problem is brought out in E. Raymond Hall's book, *Mammals of North America*. According to the author, there are 30 distinct subspecies of white-tailed deer. So you could develop a formula that works well for one subspecies but not so well for another.

For instance, in my home state of Minnesota, there are three

Although these successful hunters can guess how much this buck weighs, they will never be sure. A "deer tape" could be used to accurately estimate the buck's weight. In this chapter, the author shows you how to make your own deer tape.

subspecies—the huge *Borealis*, the western *Dacotensis* and the southeastern *Macroura*.

Another bugaboo is the overall condition of a particular deer herd. In years of mast crop abundance, the deer will have as much as three or four inches of body fat on their backs. In lean years, one or two inches of fat is typical.

So what's the answer? Simple. Use an equation that's best suited for the deer you hunt. I've already done the legwork by carefully comparing several formulas from a number of areas throughout the country, and tossing out the ones that produced the widest extremes. You should be able to come up with something that is close enough to at least settle an argument or two.

But it should still be fine-tuned on the local level. To do this, contact your state game department or conservation agency and ask them what formula they use. Then compare it to the ones listed below. Take it a step further and have your deer weighed to confirm the reliability of your equation.

To make your own "deer tape," all you need is a tape measure. So go to your nearest fabric store and purchase an ordinary yellow cloth tape measure. Then, scribble the appropriate formula on it with a permanent ink pen.

If you hunt the South, including Texas: C (circumference measured in inches of the deer's chest) x 5.6, minus 94 = field-dressed weight.

If you hunt the Midwest, particularly Minnesota, Michigan and Wisconsin: C (circumference measured in inches of deer's chest) x 7.7, minus 178 = dressed weight.

If you hunt anywhere else in North America, especially Pennsylvania: C (circumference measured in inches of deer's chest) x 6.5, minus 120 = dressed weight.

Rather than carry a calculator with you in your fanny pack, I suggest multiplying through the normal range of measurements ahead of time. Then, inscribe them on the tape measure.

Based on the Midwest formula and rounded to the nearest pound, my deer tape reads:

40-inch chest = 130-pound field-dressed deer;
41-inch chest = 138-pound field-dressed deer;
42-inch chest = 145-pound field-dressed deer;
43-inch chest = 153-pound field-dressed deer;
44-inch chest = 160-pound field-dressed deer;
45-inch chest = 169-pound field-dressed deer;
46-inch chest = 176-pound field-dressed deer;

47-inch chest = 184-pound field-dressed deer;
48-inch chest = 192-pound field-dressed deer;
49-inch chest = 199-pound field-dressed deer;
50-inch chest = 207-pound field-dressed deer;
51-inch chest = 215-pound field-dressed deer;
52-inch chest = 222-pound field-dressed deer;
53-inch chest = 230-pound field-dressed deer;
54-inch chest = 238-pound field-dressed deer;
55-inch chest = 246-pound field-dressed deer;
56-inch chest = 253-pound field-dressed deer;
57-inch chest = 261-pound field-dressed deer;
58-inch chest = 269-pound field-dressed deer;
59-inch chest = 276-pound field-dressed deer;
60-inch chest = 284-pound field-dressed deer.

The most reliable formula in the country won't do you a bit of good if your in-the-field measurements are not accurate. One research coordinator told me that even trained officials can come up with different heart girth figures if they're not careful. He suggests that you observe three rules when taking a measurement with the tape.

First, always place the tape directly behind the animal's front leg while it is on flat ground. Second, run the tape around the chest in a uniformly snug manner, perpendicular to the back. And third, make sure the chest cavity is neither compressed nor enlarged. Some hunters prop it open with a stick for better cooling after evisceration; the animal may stiffen in this position and inflate the chest measurement.

In addition to the field-dressed weight, suppose you want to know how much your deer weighed on the hoof. No problem. There are formulas for this too, although they are not quite as accurate.

If you hunt in the East, simply multiply the dressed weight by 1.25 and add four pounds. For the Midwest and West, multiply the dressed weight by 1.25 and add 2.6 pounds. For southern deer hunters, multiply the dressed weight by 1.17 and add five pounds.

And finally, there is a way to determine how much venison your deer will yield: You should get back roughly half the dressed weight of the deer, provided you didn't order a lot of sausage or hamburger.

18

Big Buck
Photo Gallery

NAHC member Jim Vaughn of Lincoln, Nebraska with the 10-point whitetail that he took near Harvard, Nebraska.

NAHC member Steve Moak of Westerlo, New York, with his 8-point whitetail taken in Cotulla, Texas.

NAHC member Neil Adams of Langhorne, Pennsylvania, with his 10-point whitetail. Neil shoots a PSE MagnaFlite bow. He arrowed this buck with a 2018 Gamegetter shaft tipped with a Rocky Mountain 4-blade broadhead.

NAHC member Mark Bisacca of Kansas City, Missouri, with the 10-point whitetail he took in Missouri.

NAHC member Kenneth Kania of Milwaukee, Wisconsin, with his 11-point whitetail. Kenneth took this buck while hunting with J&J Guide Service near Mill Iron, Montana.

Index